LESSONS
From the
CREEK

JENNIFER D. JOHNSTON

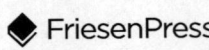 FriesenPress

Suite 300 - 990 Fort St
Victoria, BC, V8V 3K2
Canada

www.friesenpress.com

Copyright © 2020 by Jennifer D. Johnston
First Edition — 2020

All rights reserved.

No part of this publication may be reproduced in any form, or by any means, electronic or mechanical, including photocopying, recording, or any information browsing, storage, or retrieval system, without permission in writing from FriesenPress.

ISBN
978-1-5255-6610-3 (Hardcover)
978-1-5255-6611-0 (Paperback)
978-1-5255-6612-7 (eBook)

1. SELF-HELP

Distributed to the trade by The Ingram Book Company

For Joey; You are a shining star in a world so full of darkness. I am eternally grateful for all the ways in which you shine on me.

— Kanga

TABLE OF CONTENTS

ABOUT THE CREEK	v
ABOUT THE LESSONS	viii
LESSON 1	1
LESSON 2	6
LESSON 3	12
LESSON 4	18
LESSON 5	25
LESSON 6	30
LESSON 7	34
LESSON 8	40
LESSON 9	45
LESSON 10	50
LESSON 11	55
LESSON 12	61
LESSON 13	67
LESSON 14	72
LESSON 15	76
LESSON 16	83
LESSON 17	88
LESSON 18	92
LESSON 19	98
LESSON 20	103
LESSON 21	108
LESSON 22	113
LESSON 23	117
LESSON 24	122
LESSON 25	126
FINAL SENTIMENTS FROM THE CREEK	130

ABOUT THE CREEK

I live in a beautiful small town in the Niagara region of Ontario. We moved here fourteen years ago when my ex-husband and I came to open a running store and training business. It has been my home ever since. There are many things to love about this place, including the sense of community, the amenities and the close proximity to anything a family (with or without children) could require. I often tell people that moving to this small town probably saved my younger daughter's life, and I still believe that. My grandson had the opportunity to grow up in the same intimate, supportive community for the first years of his life, and for that I am grateful. I received a great deal of love and support (financial and emotional) during my recent diagnosis, treatment, and recovery from a very rare form of skin cancer.

On occasion, tourists would stop in to our running store to look at shoes. When they would comment about how they thought our town seemed like a great place to live, we would agree but quickly tell them that they probably wouldn't like it. We wanted to keep our small town small! The people here are like family. They'll give you a piece of their mind but also a piece of their heart. There is a real hub of positive energy here, and I am so thankful to be a part of it.

What I love most about our spot on the Niagara Peninsula is the natural beauty that surrounds and infuses this place. There is nowhere in Niagara where the escarpment is closer to Lake Ontario. Our town sits on the breathtaking Canadian lakeshore of one of the most beautiful members of the Great Lakes. It is nestled in an area rich with thousands of trees, at the foot of an escarpment that overlooks the town like a proud parent. The weather can change every kilometre or so, and the climate supports grapes and other tender fruits like nowhere else on earth.

The Bruce Trail (an 885 km long trail that runs from Tobermory, at the tip of the Bruce Peninsula, to Niagara Falls) and its side trails crisscross the town in every direction. On many of these trails, one will cross or travel beside Forty Mile Creek—the creek that graced me with the lessons in this book.

Nature in general, and water specifically, have always provided lessons, if we look for them. We are the same in so many ways. The ocean is made up of countless water droplets, just as humanity is made up of countless souls. As different as we feel we may be, we are really the same, because we all come from the same ocean. When we work together, we can become nations or social movements, just as water droplets working together can become waves or currents. We have the potential to work together for the greater good, just as water droplets have the potential to work together to water our planet.

Unfortunately, there is also potential for negative outcomes, such as oppressive tyrannies or mass genocide, just as water droplets can also form floods or tidal waves. The progress of water can produce significant and lasting changes in the landscape by its slow and steady interaction with its surroundings, such as the Grand Canyon. People have accomplished this also, in situations like the Great Wall of China and the pyramids of Giza. Together, we are capable of creating amazing technological and humanitarian advances. Together, we are on the edge of a great spiritual awakening, bringing higher consciousness to humanity as a whole.

We are not so different in our adherence to certain laws of nature. Water will almost always behave the same way in the same circumstances, because water's behaviour is dependent on it being water, not on the circumstances. Humanity has a history of behaving the same way in similar circumstances, because our behaviour depends on the fact that we're human, not on the circumstances.

This book explores the similarities between humans and water droplets, what we can learn from them in order to become better at expressing our authentic selves, and more aligned to our true purpose as souls having a human experience here in this physical reality.

As I mentioned, I gained the insights that I offer here from Forty Mile Creek, which is not so named for its length but rather for its distance from the Niagara River. The creek tumbles down the Niagara escarpment at Beamer's Falls and wends its way through beautiful forests and a bustling little town to eventually empty into Lake Ontario.

The creek has many different facets. It supports parks, trails, willows, wildlife, fish and thousands of birds. It has loaned its name to a local Canadian Whiskey Distillery. Its banks give countless dogs a bouquet of new smells to explore on their daily walks. It gives local teens a place to hang out with friends and break some rules. My grandson and I always enjoy walking along the bank-side trails, throwing rocks, looking for fish and learning about nature. It has given me numerous places to meditate, think, dream, and perhaps most importantly, it has inspired the lessons in this book.

ABOUT THE LESSONS

I have always been drawn to water, and I know I'm not alone. Who among us hasn't been dragged out of some lake, pool, or pond as a child in the summertime, kicking and screaming because we didn't want to get out, even though our lips were turning blue? This happened to me quite often, and I still enjoy swimming outside. Rain soothes my soul and the babbling of a book or stream can inject a bit of peace and calm into the most stressful of days. Deep soaker tubs have become pretty much standard issue in most newly built homes. Hot-tub sales have skyrocketed in recent years, and many women now elect to have water births, because it is considered a more natural way to bring new life into the world.

Physically speaking, our bodies are made up of at least 80 to 90 percent water, and the nature of water can show us the wisdom of our hearts as well as our bodies. Calm bodies of water were used as the first mirrors, and water has the ability to reflect not only our physical appearance but the state of our emotional bodies as well. A Japanese scientist named Masaru Emoto (1943- 2014) performed numerous experiments where jars of water were blessed, labelled with different emotions, like love, anger, peace and hate, or received directed thoughts (positive and negative). His findings were striking, because when samples of water from each of the bottles were frozen and the water crystallized, the slides representing the various thoughts and emotions looked quite different. The bottles labelled with positive thoughts, blessings, and positive emotions produced magnificent crystals as the water samples froze, while the samples of water from the jars that were subject to negative thoughts, or labelled with negative emotions, produced no organized crystals. Our emotional and physical bodies respond to thoughts and emotions in a similar fashion, withering when subjected to negative thoughts and emotions and thriving with prolonged exposure to positive thoughts and emotions.

So many great cultures throughout history have believed that not only do we have a direct connection to nature, but that humans are actually an inextricable part of nature, as crucial to the planet as trees or the sun. They believe that this relationship is meant to be a mutually beneficial one, where the earth feeds us and we care for the earth in return. As the earth groans with the weight of trying to sustain us in increasing numbers, the human race has dropped the ball on our end, through our abuse, neglect and exploitation. The earth keeps up her part of the deal, feeding us to the point of exhaustion. This sustenance includes food for our bodies but also food for our souls, if we choose to partake in the bounty offered.

For time immemorial, great minds have found infinite wisdom in nature. Consider such peoples as the Incans, Mayans, Tibetan monks, Maoris, Australian Aboriginals, and Native Americans and their use of astronomy, herbs and various forms of meditation. In recent years, we have started revisiting and consulting ancient practices, such as Chinese and Ayurvedic medicines. Just yesterday, as I perused the aisles at my local drugstore for vitamins, I marvelled at the vast selection of naturally sourced supplements. There are now almost as many herbal remedies available as the mainstream, pharmaceutically developed treatments.

I am thrilled that the western world is currently graduating more naturopaths, homeopaths, osteopaths, and chiropractors than ever before. Health-insurance companies often cover treatments such as massage, reflexology and Reiki. Movies like *Avatar* and *Arrival* encourage us to consider that there is more, both "out there" and right here, under our noses.

Avatar depicts a race on a distant planet where all the inhabitants respect themselves, each other, vegetation, wildlife and the planet as a whole. The wisest members of their society are trees, not people or animals, and everything on the planet is connected through tree roots, which transmit electromagnetic impulses and thoughts which can be shared between individuals regardless of species. In the end, the intruders (humans, there to pillage all of the planet's natural resources for profit), are banished because every living thing on the planet bands together to battle the common threat.

In the movie *Arrival*, "pods" of an alien ship land in numerous major centres on earth in a non-threatening way, but their method of communication is completely foreign to us. The alien race still manages to encourage us, as a people (all of humanity as ONE people), to put aside our differences and work together to affect a positive outcome.

Ralph Waldo Emmerson and Henry David Thoreau, both nineteenth century transcendentalist authors, encouraged us to keep a simple, uncluttered connection, thus launching a whole social movement known as minimalism. Minimalists have had enough of the excessive materialism associated with capitalist society and strive to reduce that extravagance by limiting their use of technology, their number of possessions and their waste. Thoreau's *On Walden Pond* became the "how-to manual" for people who wanted to simplify, de-clutter, and reprioritize the importance of material things in their lives.

These insights, while being timely and pertinent to today's issues and complexities, are not new. Currently, we have an over-abundance of knowledge and an incredible lack of wisdom. We can apply this growing movement toward simplicity and minimalism to our education system as well. What do we need to teach our children so as best to equip them for adult life? What do we *need* to know? Well, I would say firstly, ourselves, secondly, the other people with whom we share our lives, and thirdly, what surrounds us every day. I like to refer to this as the "meditate, communicate, and observe" method of education.

If, after a thorough exploration of these three areas, we want to discuss more traditional subjects, such as physics and grammar, great! I'm not saying that self-knowledge is the only knowledge necessary. It's more about prioritizing than exclusivity. Self-knowledge is the crucial basis of any education, because once we know ourselves, we have insight into everyone and everything we share atoms with. We have the wisdom of the ages within us, we just need to be taught to ask and then reminded how to listen.

We need to learn how to discern what problems and illusions we have created ourselves, by comparing our experience to the patterns that occur repeatedly in nature. Only then can we correct our errors and misunderstandings. This approach is being integrated into our education system with increasing regularity.

The Maharishi school in Fairfield, Iowa, teaches transcendental meditation as a method of governing our own thoughts and feelings. They also teach from the platform that everything is connected. The children who attend this school are happy and well-adjusted because they know themselves, their environment and their role in that environment. Many inner-city schools have also started employing meditation practices to help students manage their emotions, so that they are better behaved in social situations and better able to focus in a classroom setting.

Simple solutions can often tackle complex problems, so the lessons in this book are pretty straight forward. The following points are some tips on how to digest this wisdom in a way that speaks to you and stays with you after you finish the book:

1. Read through the whole book first, if you like. You might find particular lessons that seem especially pertinent in your present life, so you may want to bookmark these lessons. There a few references to previous lessons, and some later lessons build on the ones before, so it's best to tackle them in order. Plan to focus on one lesson at a time without a schedule, although I usually recommend at least a week with each one. Take it as slowly as you like to give yourself time to mull each lesson over, discover different applications for different areas of your life, and really make each lesson your own. Some realisations only reveal themselves with time, so don't rush.

2. It's best to do the lessons in order, and don't avoid any of them either. If you find yourself thinking, as you read a particular lesson, *Well yeah! Of course!* or *That's a load of crap!* … watch those lessons! Take some time and sit with those ones. If you find yourself experiencing either of those reactions, or you feel yourself procrastinating, it means that the lesson speaks to you and probably touches on something you'd rather not bring out into the light. You need to give those lessons some special attention. Resistance is a sure sign of a buried truth, and our defences can jump into action before we even know what we're missing!

3. There has been a lot of chatter about journaling in the self-help type books and publications that have come out in the past couple decades. The reason for this chatter is that journaling works! Once you have

read a lesson and digested the content, think about areas where it might apply in the present landscape of your life. Meditation is a great help in spending some time with your thoughts on a lesson. Work some stuff through. Think of some changes you would like to see as you shed some light on the dark parts you usually keep hidden during any self-examination. Keep your focus on what you can change going forward, rather than regretting what you did in the past. You will be able to read the same lesson again six months from now and glean completely different information, due to whatever is then at the forefront of your current life events. Like the creek, the available insights will continue to flow.

4. Acceptance and goal setting. We will touch on this in Lesson 13. The gist is "accept where you are, but don't be so satisfied that you're tempted to stay there." You are exactly where you're supposed to be at this point in your life, but you're not meant to live there indefinitely. Gratitude for what you have is crucial, but it does not preclude aspirations for something better. Wanting to evolve does not mean you disrespect where you are. What next? Your life will only change when you do.

5. The journal prompts at the end of each chapter are just that, prompts. Try to do those exercises, because they will encourage you in the uncomfortable direction of growth, but also feel free to write about whatever comes up as you work through the exercises. Take some time to just dump whatever's in your heart and head out onto the page.

In conclusion, please enjoy the book! You are about to be made privy to some simple yet versatile insights into the nature of our Universe, as seen looking down from the banks of a small-town creek. I usually write things down to solidify ideas in my head, but I've been amazed at how little of this book I remember after writing it. It truly wrote itself, and the only thing I feel comfortable taking credit for is holding the pen (I wrote the entire first copy long hand, in cursive, in a school notebook). I look forward to reading it with you, and revisiting all the lessons, to be reminded of what we once knew but have since forgotten.

LESSON 1:

YOU ARE A THING OF BEAUTY NO MATTER WHAT KIND OF SHIT IS ALL AROUND YOU.

Each of us is uniquely beautiful. I know, I know. If you've read anything that even vaguely resembles a self-help book, numerous Facebook posts, seen talk shows, etc., you've heard this before. What does it mean? I get up most mornings, look in the mirror, and think, *That can't be right! I don't remember getting hit by a truck last night!*

I'm a bit overweight right now. I'm fifty-three years old. I'm missing the better part of my right eyebrow due to a good-sized scar. My ex-husband left me last year for a younger, thinner, richer woman, and I have a *lot* of laugh lines! What surrounds my soul (who I truly am on the inside), doesn't appeal to me sometimes. Recent life events have taken a toll on what was already shaky self-confidence. But I still look in the mirror every day, and say to that beautiful soul looking back at me, "Good Morning, gorgeous!" because my authentic self *is* gorgeous, no matter how I view the appearance of the physical body I see—the one I am so quick to judge.

Forty Mile Creek runs right through the middle of our town, as I mentioned in "About the Creek." What I didn't mention is that it runs directly between the Lions Club Pool parking lot and the back of the Food Basics Plaza—not even the front of the plaza- the back, where all the dumpsters are, where the transport-truck bays are located, and the diesel fumes fill the air. Yet, it was in that exact spot that the creek gave over this first lesson.

In the midst of the noise, fumes, asphalt, garbage, and traffic, it revealed its timeless beauty, simplicity, and wisdom to me. Even surrounded by all that crap, the creek is remarkable, and so are you. Your story has made you the remarkable person you are, and it doesn't matter if that authentic you is surrounded by a pudgy or aging body, older clothes, scars, a bad temper or a few wrinkles. All of these things are results of your experience, and you are *not* your body. You even exist beyond your "negative" personality traits and coping mechanisms. You are a beautiful soul made of light, love, stardust and eternal wisdom.

Do you remember the story and picture of the Afghan girl with the amazing sea-green eyes that appeared on the cover of National Geographic in June of 1985? That photo took the world by storm and was referred to as "the first world's third-world Mona Lisa". The photographer, Steve McCurry, and a team from National Geographic managed to locate her (named Sharbat Gula), in 2002 and told the story of her very difficult life. At the time her picture was taken in 1984, she was an orphan of war, living in a Pakistani refugee camp. Few of us can appreciate the horror of her life, but that picture sparked the reactions of millions of people around the world, because of her stark beauty. She was living in a refugee camp, as an orphan of a terrible war! There is no question that she was surrounded by shit ... but beautiful, nonetheless.

Many of us allow ourselves, through our own choices, to become victims of our environment. We ask ourselves, "What's the use? Why should we even try, when our surroundings are so dismal and constricting?" The truth is that you are beautiful and those dismal surroundings are a great backdrop for you to really shine!

My father used to go to a crappy little gas station near our house, even though the gas was a bit more expensive there. The main reason he continued to give the owner his business was the staff. They would always greet him with an enthusiastic "Good morning/afternoon/evening!" and chat and sing while they pumped his gas. They worked at a menial job that most people would consider beneath them, and they were as happy as larks. They made their customers happy as well, because they expressed their beauty in what most people would consider a less-than-ideal profession. They were joyous, and their ability to be true to themselves gave their customers permission to be true to their own selves as well. Their authenticity allowed and encouraged their patrons' authenticity. Without pretence or ego, those workers were able to get through to their customers' inner selves. They were able to share their joy with their customers before the customers remembered that they had an exterior that they weren't fond of or happy with. Many patrons would start smiling and singing along before they realized what they were doing. What an amazing gift these workers were able to give so many people!

Think of a few characteristics that you admire most about some of your favourite people. When you can appreciate qualities in other people, it makes it easier to accept and appreciate the qualities you possess. It's like training yourself to look for positive things, and this is an invaluable skill because you really do find what you look for. Think about how you might have a few of those traits you admire. Think about what you love about your friends and family members. Think of things you like about yourself or things other people have complimented you on. Think about what you feel is "the real inner you," if you felt safe and didn't need the defences that your experience has necessitated you build. Thinking of yourself as a child can help with this part.

All of this is key!!! We have been conditioned in our society that "blowing our own horn" makes us conceited or arrogant. Arrogance and conceit usually stem from insecurity, not confidence. Knowing your qualities and being happy about them, as well as knowing your faults and accepting them, fosters confidence, not conceit. If you can't think of what qualities you might possess (because we're not encouraged to do that), think about the nice things that others have said to you. If you hesitate or feel yourself resisting ("I don't actually have to write a list!" or "people have complimented me, but they don't really *know* me!" or "I can't think of anything!" are all methods of resistance), you need to focus on this exercise even more!

If the first words out of your mouth are "Yeah, but..." or "This is just silly," stop right there, and think of another thing that's good about you. You tell yourself you don't like you and exactly what you feel your faults are all the time. It hasn't helped, and you don't need any more practice at that! Surrender that garbage to the Universe. Write all your usual self-criticisms on a piece of paper and then burn that sucker! Give up your hold on the negative. Quite often, we use our faults as an excuse for bad behaviour or inaction: "I can't help it, it's just the way I am." or "this trauma happened to me _ years ago, and I haven't been the same since." or my personal favourite, "When I was young, my parents did…"

I am not trivializing the devastating effects of some of life's traumatic experiences; I'm saying you have a choice every minute of every day, so choose the positive. Don't even worry about trying to eliminate the negative thoughts, because this will keep your focus on them. It's like telling yourself you're not going to get sick over and over again; the focus is still "sick." Grow the positive. Just for a change, figure out the good things about you and think about those. That is where you want your focus!

Once you have a list of good points going, think about how you could show these points more often. How can you use these newly recognized qualities in your everyday life? The best way to build a muscle is to exercise it. The best way to become comfortable and competent is practice. You can even play out some situations in your head, so you can be prepared to be fabulous. Try out your "new you" anonymously at first, if you're afraid of what the people around you are going to say (although they will probably be ecstatic that you're happier if they really care about you). Change can be uncomfortable, even when you're trying to change in a good way, so take baby steps.

As you change, your environment can't help but change as well. Feed some birds, compliment a complete stranger on something they're wearing, or donate food to the local food bank. Signing a cheque or donating online doesn't have the same effect. Andrrea Hess, developer of a healing modality known as Soul Realignment, tells us that decision is thought, choice is action, and karma is reaction. Good choices equal good karma, so action is key. *Go* to your community thrift store and donate, *visit* the older man on your street who lives alone, *make* a casserole for the lady at work who just had surgery, *drop* a card in the mail to someone you haven't seen in ages because snail mail is still awesome…

Try something that challenges you a little. You will feel great! The people on the receiving end will also feel great! And you will probably feel inspired to sport the "new you" to the ones you were nervous about at the beginning.

You can make someone's day just by saying something like, "Wow! I love your blouse!" and you'll feel good too! You might not get to perfect the first day, but you'll be heading in the right direction. Our authentic selves are like the little children that we truly are: innocent and radiant. The "new you" is really the old you before you built all your walls and let yourself become jaded by what you perceived as "bad" experiences. Have your defences kept you from pain or just from joy? In my experience, pain can get at you no matter what. Joy waits to be invited in. So, let loose your beautiful self! A crumpled twenty-dollar bill is still worth twenty dollars! You may still have a couple warts, but it doesn't mean your good points aren't good anymore. Your faults don't negate the beauty of your qualities, just like the creek is still beautiful behind the Food Basics Plaza.

THE JOURNAL:

Write down five different things you like about you every day. Yep! *Every day!* Yes, you can!

Write down one way you could use, demonstrate, or put into action each of those traits.

Example: I think I have a warm smile. I could use this by smiling at someone at the office or the gym or the grocery store.

LESSON 2:

SOMETIMES SOMETHING THAT SEEMS HORRIFIC, LIKE A FLOOD OR TORRENTIAL DOWNPOUR, CAN ACTUALLY SPEED UP THE PROGRESS TOWARD YOUR GOAL.

THE GOAL FOR THE CREEK IS THE LAKE. FOR YOU, IT MAY BE ENLIGHTENMENT, INNER PEACE, FULFILLMENT, HAPPINESS, OR SOMETHING ELSE ALTOGETHER.

Everyone these days seems to be talking about the adverse effects of stress. "Stress kills" and "stress relief" are phrases that can be heard almost daily. So many people claim that stress is the enemy. People often have to take time off work for stress leave. The occurrence of health concerns like tension headaches, self-medication, digestive issues and ulcers is rampant in our society. We, as humans, tend to take things to the extreme, and our aversion to stress is no exception. The truth is that stress is not bad. Our addiction to it, exposure to too much of it, and our obsession with jumping through all manner of hoops to avoid it, are what's bad. Nothing changes without stress.

We get pushed, we get pulled, and suddenly our lives change. Our shape changes, our comfort level changes, and maybe, just maybe, we grow a little.

In the past decade or so, humankind has made massive advancements in technology and athletic performance. Some of our fellow water droplets are achieving feats which seem super-human. Some people have not only broken through what were thought to be the upper limits of human capabilities, they have blasted through them. When questioned, they will attribute their ability to do the seemingly impossible to being in a state of "flow", just like water in a creek! Also known as 'the zone' or 'runner's high', this is a state of being completely in the moment. Many have recounted tales of time slowing almost to a stop and being in a state of hyper-awareness while experiencing this 'flow state'. Those who have experienced flow, would do almost anything to get there again. Occasionally, a state similar to flow can be artificially (and imperfectly) reproduced by drugs or alcohol, and the pursuit of recreating even the poorest imitation of that feeling can easily lead to addiction. In any case, it has been scientifically proven that one of the main conditions that precipitates a state of flow, is stress. Once in the flow state, the stress disappears and one is left feeling that the present moment is everything, and that they are one with that everything.

On the other hand, most of us have become abnormally attached to (maybe even obsessed with) maintaining the status quo. We mistakenly call it "peace", but peace can certainly exist in a climate of change. The status quo cannot. Can you imagine if we never acquiesced to the "stress" of potty training? *No! My parents have unreasonable expectations of me, and society has put too much pressure on me. So, I'm going to medicate, meditate, drink, and buy really big diapers.* This example, as well as many others in life, makes us realize that growth (physical and spiritual) is impossible without at least a bit of stress.

Now don't get me wrong, people have also developed an inability to set healthy boundaries. They then may have to deal with too much self-induced stress as a result of trying to meet unreasonable work, family or friend demands, because they refuse to take on the initial stress of saying no. Anything ignored seldom goes away, and trying to avoid the initial, relatively minor stress of saying no to someone can lead to a much greater and less manageable stress of actually having to do something that is onerous, taxing and overly time consuming. Stress, as it is meant to function in our bodies, is an alert or a call to change something. If you are addicted to the adrenaline a stressful situation unleashes in your body, you are a lot less likely to resolve the situation and much more likely to get yourself into an emotional knot, just to keep the train rolling.

If you feel stress and you make a change, the stress will subside. If you feel stress and you spend a lot of energy analyzing the situation, dwelling on how unfair it is, deciding what your choices are and worrying about the future, nothing changes and the stress continues. This is decision (thought) versus choice (action), and this condition is not sustainable!

So... where does this leave us? Most times, when something terrible happens, such as job loss, illness or accident, we're sure that life, as we know it, is about to end. Yes, it is, and hallelujah for that!!! Stress will push us to change, and if we refuse, it will often just keep pushing harder. Life events like breakdowns, illnesses or financial disasters are rarely things that "come out of the blue." In my own case, I literally had years of warning signs and feeling like I was in a life trap, but the signs and feelings were just too inconvenient to heed.

We couldn't just close our store! Well, as it happens, we could and we did! I couldn't go back to school at my age! Um... yes, I could, and I did that too! But we won't have any money! Really? None? Well, not *enough* money. Oh no? Enough money for what, exactly? To eat? To keep a roof over our heads? Well, with a budget we could have enough money for that stuff.

So, what was the problem? I was letting my fear dress up as a desire to avoid stress in my life. "I'm too... old/tired/broke/successful... for this" is just one of the many classic costumes that fear wears to render us stagnant—trapped—but still not free from stress! The stress continues to creep in as we are hounded by what we think of as options: the options of changing or staying the same.

"I would like to do that, but I can't just quit my job!"

"I should go to the gym, but I'm so tired when I get home from work."

"I would love to take that course, but I can't be out every Tuesday night. What about the kids?"

Stress loses its power when you choose to take action, when you're immersed in what you're doing, and approach it with unbridled enthusiasm and reckless abandon. If we refuse, many times the dam breaks, and we have a flood on our hands.

My first flood was my cancer diagnosis and the rarity of my particular type of the disease. The consequences? We closed a dying business and kept the part that brought us joy. My younger daughter and I opened a Vegan Bistro to help spread the lessons that we learned regarding food as it relates to health. I found a great energy healer (or rather, he found me!), wrote a book, and got my commercial helicopter pilot's licence.

My second flood was the failure of a relationship that I was sure would last forever. It turned my world upside down, and I struggled for months to recover. As a result, I embarked on a journey of self-awareness and discovery of my soul's true purpose. Now I have the opportunity to tour with my book, guide people to reconcile with their true spiritual journey and help people in less fortunate situations, because I was unable to stay put in my "comfortable" yet unfulfilling relationship. A couple of these things may have happened eventually, but it would have taken awhile. A couple of these things probably wouldn't have happened at all, and I would not have reached my "lake" in this lifetime.

I used to hear or read about people who were diagnosed with a terrible disease or who had survived a horrific accident, and they swore they were thankful for what had happened to them. I would think, *Bullshit! I mean, kudos to you for making the best of a bad situation, but you can't possibly actually be grateful for this misfortune that has befallen you!* Now, after surviving a few of my own floods, I get it. I would not be where I am now without those floods. I understand how those experiences got me here, and given the chance, I wouldn't change a thing. It's about reaching a level of peace.

Peace is another thing I hear a *lot* of people talking about lately. Like the answer to avoiding stress is creating peace by eliminating people, things, drama, etc. from their lives to attain that elusive state of peace. It's like they think peace is something you create outside to protect your equilibrium inside. To me, creating a rock solid, unshakable equilibrium inside means you don't have to worry about what happens (much of which we can't control anyway) outside. Some call it living in joy, some call it detachment, some call it being stress free, but whatever you call it, it is the only way of being free to offer ourselves to this experience rather than protecting ourselves from it. That protection can become a cage and a source of stress in a heartbeat, and that's fear, not peace at all.

In times that threaten my state of peace by inciting a stress reaction, I often think of an ancient Chinese proverb about a poor man living in a small village. He borrowed money from his neighbours to purchase a stallion, in hopes of making money breeding the horse to local mares. The day after he got the stallion, he awoke to find that, during the night, the horse had escaped. All his neighbours came around saying, "Oh, this is awful! Your stallion got away and you still owe us money!" to which the man said, "Good thing, bad thing ... who knows?"

The man decided to go out in search of the stallion and returned later that afternoon with the stallion and six or seven mares that the stallion had taken up with. This time, the villagers all said, "Oh, fortune has smiled on you! Now you have a whole herd of horses! How lucky you are!" Again, the man answered, "Good thing, bad thing ... who knows?"

The very next day, the man's son was riding one of the mares to try and break her to saddle. The mare bucked the boy off, and he broke his leg quite badly. All the neighbours came around and said, "Oh, what an awful turn of luck! Now your boy will be disfigured, and no one will want to marry him!" Once again, the man said, "Good thing, bad thing ... who knows?"

Several weeks later, the conscription gangs came to the village, because the country had gone to war, and the emperor ordered the service of all able-bodied young men in the country. All the young men in the man's village were taken, except his son, because of his injured leg. All the villagers came to the man again and said, "Fortune has truly smiled on you. All our sons have been taken to fight in this terrible war, but you still have your boy here with you!" Once again, the man responded, "Good thing, bad thing ... who knows?"

This story could go on and on, but the point is that events aren't bad or good until we decide how to respond to them. Sometimes an event that looks awful can precipitate amazing things!

If you have a flood, ride it out. Practice doing things that accentuate the qualities you discovered that you liked about yourself in the last lesson. Tread water so you don't drown. Surround yourself with loving people who really care about you and will support you. Try not to let circumstances around you turn you into someone you don't care for. Breathe. It might be the best thing that has ever happened to you, even if it takes some time to see it. Just because you can't see it right now, doesn't mean something great isn't happening behind the scenes. Look for your flow state.

If you feel like the flood is sending you backwards, just remember that, when you've taken a wrong turn, often the fastest way to get back on the right track is to go back the way you came. Maybe you've asked the Universe for happiness, and you're not going to get it working for the company you're working for now. Maybe you've asked for inner peace, but you won't voluntarily stop running like a hamster in a wheel. Maybe you have to stop asking how you can get what you want from your life and start asking how you can *change* your life to get what you want. Sometimes, the only way to recreate that state of flow or get to the place you want to be in your life is to be carried by a flood.

THE JOURNAL:

Recall some stressful times in your life and a few things you learned as a result of going through those hard times. Look for positives, and you will find some. Be grateful for those lessons. Feeling gratitude for the lessons lessens any pain that you may still feel from the memories. Once you can remember with gratitude, the memory becomes experience, and wisdom comes from experience. Recall an occasion when time stood still, everything seemed to click, and you were in a state of flow: during a piano recital, your best round of golf, watching the sunset with your spouse or partner. Know that your present stress can herald that feeling again, and lean in.

Hike in Montana

LESSON 3:

SOMETIMES THAT BIG STRESS, LIKE A FLOOD OR TORRENTIAL DOWNPOUR, CAN GIVE YOU UNEXPECTED COMPANY ON YOUR JOURNEY.

SHARING THE EXPERIENCE WITH OTHER WATER DROPLETS IN THE CREEK, CAN HELP YOU RECOGNIZE AND ATTAIN YOUR GOAL.

If you are going through an issue, problem, addiction or a disease, there's a pretty good chance that you can find a support group for your specific challenge somewhere. The major reason for the recent popularity of the support-group phenomenon is that these groups work! People need people who understand their situation via first-hand experience. There is *huge* comfort in knowing that you're not alone. There are also huge benefits to sharing a knowledge base or getting tips from someone who has already "been there, done that."

If your flood is not a personally specific flood (think mass lay-offs or natural disaster, etc.), you almost automatically get thrown into a group of people who already have a pretty good idea of what you're going through, so *share!* You will handle parts of this better than others, and others will handle different parts better than you, so combine forces and share the benefits of your strengths. Receive the benefits of other people's strengths. Many people feel that "being strong" means not needing help, but there is more strength in numbers. It's a much stronger position to recognize your weaknesses and ask for help in those areas than it is to ignore and deny those weaknesses and have them come back to bite you on the ass!

Even if your flood is specific to you, such as job loss or injury, there really isn't much new under the sun, and there *will* be someone somewhere who can relate. This is not said to belittle the experience or trauma, just to reiterate that, no matter what you're going through, chances are, someone within reach has gone through something similar. Get their angle, copy their coping mechanisms, join their Facebook group…Find your tribe!

Times like these demonstrate that we don't benefit from separation. There are many age-old adages, such as "together we stand, divided we fall" and "there's no I in team." These adages exist because they're true too. Even if you can't find people in the exact same boat, find people who share your ideals, your beliefs or your style. They may be able to think clearly while your mind is cluttered or preoccupied. They may not be engulfed in the same emotional turmoil, and if they think in a similar way to you otherwise, they may be able to offer you an *"Ah-ha!"* moment when you can't quite see through the fog of your emotions. There are many drops in the creek with whom you already share other things in common; find out what they think they would do in your shoes.

I like vegan chili. I make it all the time, and because I do, I just throw all the stuff in a crock pot in the morning, leave it cooking all day and enjoy it for dinner with a crusty bun. If I wanted to make my daughter's famous vegan ranch dressing, I would need to follow a recipe or ask her how to make it, because she makes it all the time and I don't. I don't think any of us would think twice about asking a friend for a recipe. I don't think any of us would think twice about hiring a plumber or an electrician to do work we don't have the skill-set to complete ourselves. Some things are okay to DIY, but the tricky or important tasks are things we need to leave to someone with experience.

When it comes to mental health or personal issues though, our willingness to ask for help goes right out the window. Needing help with things around the house or fixing your car is nothing to be ashamed of, and needing help to cope with personal/mental health issues, such as job loss, marital break-up, addiction, or physical illness really shouldn't be any different. They're certainly tricky and important, and their occurrence isn't a sign of weakness; it's a sign that you're living your life.

I have heard repeatedly that our society of old didn't need therapists because we actually had friends we could talk to in times of distress. I'm not saying that seeing a therapist isn't a good idea. I see two on a regular basis, and they have helped me immensely. If you are struggling and have the opportunity and availability, I highly recommend you do the same. Talking to an expert can be helpful in most situations, but talk to your friends too. You may or may not know what they've been through, and you opening up about your difficulties may help them feel comfortable doing the same. Admitting that you're vulnerable reduces the degree of separation between us and our friends who love us.

There is no substitute for the energy that flows all around and between people who love each other. That energy can start healing what's broken or damaged in you, and it flows outward to change your experience outside yourself as well. Our thoughts really do shape our reality, but I will go into this a little more as we go along. In addition to that energy, talking to people in some type of formal or informal support group is an invaluable resource, because they've been there. They may become friends, kindred spirits or your biggest fans. Groups like AA and MADD are so successful for this exact reason. If we share what we know, we don't each have to learn the same lessons on our own.

There are three caveats: 1) You need to beware of becoming too dependent; 2) You need to beware of the "crabs-in-a-bucket mentality;" and 3) You need to remember that the behaviours and attitudes you adopt while trying to survive and recover, will not serve you when you are ready to flourish and grow again.

In the first case, support groups are meant to help you with your recovery, not do your recovery for you. It does no good to substitute one addiction for another or create a dependence where there wasn't one. You don't have to recover all on your own, but you do have to own your recovery. You can meet people in a support group who may become friends for life, but they can't maintain the same role in your life. A good support group will want to see you be successful at your recovery and that will involve you needing them less. If your group encourages you to fly, it's probably a healthy, truly supportive group.

In the second case, a group can really help, but if they're not offering true support (helping you get better), they may be there just to commiserate. This is the epitome of the "victim mentality" that so many people have fallen prey to these days. As I said in Lesson 1, I'm not belittling anyone's trauma as a result of awful life-experiences; I'm saying it's too easy to over-identify with that trauma and forget that you are not your experiences. You are the one who grows and shines as a result of those experiences.

You can recognize these individuals because your recovery will offend them. Just because they're offended doesn't mean they're right. They may criticize how you're doing your recovery by suggesting you're in denial. While it's true that you cannot successfully bury your past, it shouldn't bury you either. They draw energy from reliving their past traumas, and they won't want to see you get better, because then they have no excuse not to do the same. This is what's known as the crabs-in-a-bucket mentality. If you have a number of crabs in a bucket and one looks like it might crawl out over the edge, quite often the other crabs will pull the one ambitious crab back down into the bucket. In human terms, this happens when it's not necessarily outsiders holding individuals back from success, it's their peers.

In the third case, recovery is an imperative part of growth, but it is not the only part. Many people have to go through chemo to treat cancer. They don't continue the chemo when they're in remission. When I was recovering from the devastation caused by my husband's affair, I used to pat myself on the back every morning just for getting out of bed. At that time, it truly was a big accomplishment! I was treading water, trying not to drown. I couldn't even imagine trying to swim! Those baby steps were crucial for me to get back on my feet, but if I ever wanted to run again, baby steps were not enough. When you're lost and you finally find a group you identify with, there can be a temptation to stay, because you don't want to feel lost again. When you're crossing the river to a new you, support groups are like islands. Use them for a break, not somewhere to live. Unless you want to stay in a group to help others, the island is a step along the way, not your destination.

So, make the most of the company you find during challenging times, but choose your supporters carefully. Beware of people who are comfortable in their misery or distress. If someone offers you criticism of how you are choosing to do things, decide how that makes you feel. Constructive criticism should feel like an *Ah-ha!* moment, whereas criticism born out of insecurity, will just make you feel inadequate or defensive. Be cognizant of those who have the "People have average lives because that's what we do, isn't it?" mentality. "That's what we all do, isn't it? We work, we pay bills, we might raise a family, and we die." That mentality sucks the life out of you. When people who think that way are not happy, they think there is something wrong with their spouses, their kids, their jobs or with them. That's not it!! There's something wrong with the "average" life! You are meant for more! None of us are so special that we, alone, are meant for greatness. We are *all* meant for greatness. Fear of this fact can paralyze some people, and in an attempt to deny or avoid their discomfort with the idea, they may try to instil that fear in you too.

Be careful who you make space for. The quickest way to get back on the path after a trauma is to recover, and you can do that by garnering some selective support. We are all droplets in this creek, and when there's a flood, be it personal or more extensive, you can bet that many other droplets are now taking or have taken the same route down the creek bed. Most want to help and will be more than willing to share current or past strategies without insisting that you take the same approach.

THE JOURNAL:

Talk to an elder or more experienced person whom you trust. Find someone who's recovered, who's living the life you want or has insight you feel you lack, regardless of gender, ethnic background, age, etc. (my youngest daughter and stepson were invaluable resources for me during my recovery). Look around and see who's taking this journey with you. Talk about what you're going through. Ask the people you decide to make space for, if they could impart one lesson about this situation or life in general, what would it be? Get them to elaborate, hear what they're saying and write that bit of gold down in your journal, so you can revisit it often.

Never dwelling on the past. Always something new to experience. (Wayne)

LESSON 4:

DIFFERENT DROPLETS MAY TAKE DIFFERENT PATHS TO THE LAKE. NONE ARE WRONG, JUST DIFFERENT.

Forty Mile Creek varies in width and depth along its path, as most creeks and rivers do. I find it calming to watch as some of the water travels along one bank or the other, over the rocks, back and forth along the uneven edges of the creek bed. Alternately, there is always a somewhat deeper, faster-moving channel that follows a more direct route, right down the middle of the creek. Both these paths take the creek water into Lake Ontario. I don't even know if the water taking the more direct route actually gets to the lake any faster than the water that seems to meander more slowly over the rocks and along the edges of the creek. The point is that neither of these paths is the "right" path. There is no one "right" way to be water in the creek.

I find that when we've been through a particularly rough patch, we tend to discount what we perceive to be the experiences of others. "What we perceive" is a pretty important part here. You may not (and probably don't) know the whole story when it's someone else's story. I also think that we can discount our own story when we feel it doesn't compare to "what we perceive" as other people's stories. Our experiences are not winner-takes-all propositions. Just because I may have been through something particularly awful doesn't mean your "less awful" experience doesn't count at all. All of our stories are unique, important and valuable. Our journey down the creek is not a competition. I'm not going to be rewarded because I got through my journey "better" than you got through yours.

Throughout this recent age of what many call Enlightenment, we hear a lot of "I'm okay, you're okay" or "you do you, and I'll do me" type of sentiments. That philosophy is great in terms of encouraging acceptance of different points of view, but I feel like many of us don't absorb that or really know what it means. Some vaguely call it liberalism. There has been a great movement in that general direction as of late, and the danger I feel that view possesses is our tendency to either become doormats or gallantly protect the "victims." This implies that we must compromise ourselves and also suggests the people we are trying to protect are, in fact, victims.

The first assessment comes from a lack of self-worth. To fix this, we need to love ourselves. This book is intended to help you do just that. The second assessment, which is pity, can only come from a place of judgement or condescension. The *Oh-you-poor-thing!* attitude is distancing and degrading. Generosity can be used as a method of self-serving manipulation by the giver, which necessitates the *givee* maintain their victim status and not recover. If we're really trying to help, the victim should not have to remain a victim just so we can feel good about ourselves and how we're helping. We all know people who identify with their victim status, but those who identify with the generous-host status are just as unhealthy. Someone who is using their generosity to feed their feeling of superiority won't want the people they're helping to fly free. If the *givee* gets better, the generous host can't continue to pat themselves on the back for the wonderful contributions they're making to the *givee's* welfare. As the *givee* strives to gain their independence, those gifts become a cage.

All of this boils down to acceptance, mutual respect and equality. Equality is what the vast majority of people think they're advocating for, but true equality is lost if we have to choose between giving up our ideals and inflicting them on others. It is also lost if I demand to be equal, but I'm not actually happy unless I'm made to feel special. Our society has turned the concept of equality into something that kind of looks like "You're no better than I am!" when what equality really means is that we are *all* amazing! We are all special, different and equal. Two plus two equals four and so does one plus three. Different equations give equal answers. True equality requires mutual respect and acceptance. It requires cooperation without competition.

I believe in my heart that I'm a liberal thinker. What that means to me is that I respect other views while not compromising my own values. This does not mean that I arbitrarily write off your ideas if they don't exactly match my ideas. It does mean that I respect your right to worship at your chosen church or love who you love, regardless of gender identification, ethnicity or shoe size. It means that I don't condemn your great idea or insight just because I didn't think of it first.

To use the creek metaphor, my journey on this side of the creek isn't any better or worse than your journey on that side of the creek. Even if it seems to me that your journey is really hard (as I perceive it), it doesn't necessarily mean that mine is any easier or harder. If I can help you on your side, as an equal, I absolutely will. What I will not do is make my offer of assistance contingent on you coming to my side of the creek and following my journey. It's my journey. I will not criticize you for sticking to your journey. It's none of my business. I will also not change the direction of my journey just to make you feel better about your journey. That's none of *your* business. If you feel that you would like to come to my side of the creek and follow the same path I'm following, I will help you as much as I can. If you would like to offer some wisdom or insight that you feel might help me on my side, I will listen with gratitude. Whether I decide to incorporate your advice or not, I will be grateful that you offered it to me.

However, if you want to come to my side of the creek and criticize, inflict your judgement-based opinion or try to change my journey, because it's not like your journey was on the other side of the creek, I'll invite you back to your side of the creek. If your journey on the other side of the creek had been so great, you probably wouldn't have ventured over to my side of the creek. If you came to my side of the creek because you were unhappy on your side, and you thought my side looked a bit better, but you insist I make my journey more like the one you just left, well that's not very sporting of you, is it? The difference lies in acceptance, respect, and detachment from the outcome.

If you *ask* (and the importance of *that* cannot be over emphasized), I will give you my best advice, considering I have not travelled your journey up until now. People with experience in the same or similar situations can offer great wisdom and insight, as discussed in Lesson 3, but objective observation from an impartial observer can be just as valuable. What you do with that advice is up to you. I find that this is a real sticking point! If I give you something, it's yours to do with as you see fit—advice included! I don't have, and should not try to have, any control over the outcome. I do have the right to stop giving you things that you won't use.

In my view, the heart of liberalism is the sharing of ideas with acceptance and respect for differing opinions or beliefs. It is my right to retain my adherence to the principles and values, which through my experience, I have come to hold dear. The journey on my side of the creek isn't the only right way to be water in the creek, but it may be the only right way for me—same for you on your side. Let's celebrate our similarities, explore and accept our differences, and learn from each other, if we can. When our paths do meet, let's just enjoy hearing different stories and being good to each other. The journey is not a competition, so let's stop trying to convince each other that our path's the best path.

The best place to start is by trying to figure out what we believe and why we believe it. It's important while doing this to remember that beliefs are not facts, and your beliefs are not who you are. You are so much more than a collection of beliefs. Do you believe in God? Why? Is it because you have seen Him at work in your life or because your parents, family and friends at church all believe? Do you believe in a capitalist society? Why? Because we live in one and how could this many people possibly be wrong? Have you taken the time to explore other philosophies like socialism or communism? Do you know why you don't believe in them? Do you believe our government is looking out for our best interests? Why? Because that's why we elect them, and they couldn't possibly be corrupt, could they?

It is my contention that most of our defensiveness regarding our belief systems comes from our own doubts and insecurities. We tend to get defensive when someone asks us a question that we're not sure we know the answer to. If we're rock solid in our belief or knowledge, and we know why, we tend to be much more tolerant of differing opinions. "I don't think you understand what I'm saying, but I'm happy to explain if you want..."

This can't be done in a condescending way or else it goes against the "mutual respect as equals" part of the lesson. If we don't identify with our opinions or beliefs, we are much more willing to hear other sides. To say, "I believe in God" says something about my beliefs (something I have), whereas "I'm a Christian" says something about who I perceive myself to be. If I do identify with my beliefs, when you offer up a different belief, I can't help but perceive that as judgement of me as a person. It's the difference between hearing "can I suggest a better way to throw a bowling ball?" and "you're a lousy bowler". The first statement addresses something I do, whereas the second addresses who I am. Often this differentiation is actually made by the one who hears, not the one speaking.

It's the same for people who identify with their profession, such as doctors, lawyers, janitors or farmers. If you disagree with my belief system or criticize my profession, it can feel like an insult to me. Then we get into a situation where I feel you are not respecting me as a person, but I have created that myself. By viewing my profession as who I am, rather than what I do, I have created my own disrespect on your behalf. Then the temptation for me is to take a personal shot at you: "Well, you've got your head in the sand if you don't believe in modern medicine!" and I have disrespected you. This can end up being a vicious cycle in a heartbeat. There is an inherent responsibility here to respectfully stick to our guns. We cannot be walked all over if we refuse to lie down. If we have done our homework and know why we believe what we believe, it removes (or at least lessens) insecurities that can lead to defensiveness. If we don't identify with our vocation or belief system, it removes the tendency for questions, criticism or a different viewpoint to become personal. If we can step back from what we desire the truth to be (because beliefs are not facts), no matter how badly we desire it, we can be less defensive and more open to seeing what the truth actually is. If we can establish self-worth that is independent of our beliefs or profession, we can be solid and assured of our own value, regardless of what opinion others may appear to hold.

Bullying is a hot topic right now, and everyone is quick to blame the bullies. Don't get me wrong, bullying should not be tolerated under any circumstances. What people forget or don't want to admit is that bullies don't become that way all on their own. They push someone around, find out it works, and then do it again. They become more powerful as they successfully push more and more people around. Is this poor behaviour on their part? Absolutely! It flies in the face of the whole mutual respect idea in a big way! Is it ALL their fault? Nope!

When people are rock solid in who they are as opposed to identifying with what they believe or what they do, bullies can't find a soft spot. Imagine a bully approaching you saying, "You're a shrimp, and you suck at football!" and you respond by chuckling and saying, "Yeah, I'm short and I can't catch, but it doesn't matter that much to me. I just like playing." The bully's power over you is gone, because you refused to give it to him or her. You are rock solid in your knowledge of who you are and realize that your value does not depend solely on your height or your athletic prowess in football. You calmly stood up for yourself in a non-aggressive way, (humour helps so much with this) so it's a win for you, but you have also helped other potential targets as well as the bully. You have relieved the bully of the viability of being the "bad guy" as an option. In their heart of hearts, no one really wants to be a jerk. We can help them avoid that by standing our ground and employing self-respect, acceptance and mutual respect. Offer appreciation, not flattery, and refuse to lie down. If the bully has had a fair bit of success using intimidation, diffusing the situation can be significantly more difficult than in the simplified example above, but I'll address this further in Lesson 12.

We are all trying to find our way in the best manner we know how. The respect we owe our fellow droplets, and the understanding of their position, becomes so much easier to manage when we are solid in our own beliefs, self-knowledge and self-respect. After all, if our destinations are the same, we'll see each other whenever we all get where we're going. We'll be better for our individual experiences when we do, because there's no one "right" way to be water in the creek.

THE JOURNAL:

Write down two or three beliefs that you hold dear and why you believe them. Note where in your experience they came from and what solidified them as beliefs. Can you think of a couple questions that someone with a different point of view might ask? Can you answer those questions as objectively as possible? Questions only have the potential to become threats when you don't know the answers. If a question makes you feel uncomfortable, notice that you're having that reaction. Try to realize that you may have just been given an indicator, directing you to a place of potential growth. Once you find a satisfactory, fact-based answer, the question won't make you feel uncomfortable anymore. Look at you, being all solid in what you believe and why you believe it! Huzzah!!

LESSON 5:

SOME PATHS MAY LOOK EASIER, BUT THEY MAY ALSO TAKE LONGER.

I mentioned in the preface that my ex-husband and I came to our town to open a running store. The "what we perceive" concept and a running analogy both help a lot with this lesson, so bear with me.

I'm a trail runner. My ex-husband really loves the feel of running down an open road, but I don't really like it. I would much rather be out in the woods. We conducted running clinics for runners of all skill levels, and when we had our store, we also started to offer "introduction to trail-running" workshops on Friday nights. As you might expect, lesson number one was pick up your feet! Lesson number two (which brings in what we learned from the last lesson) was don't feel you have to follow the person in front of you. They may jump some big tree roots or branches and take a more difficult route than you feel comfortable with. If that works, they may get to the end of the trail faster than you. If that doesn't work, they could sprain an ankle and need a wheelbarrow to carry them out of the woods. You may take a short side trail around a boulder, which looks easier, but it might take you longer. Neither way is the right way. I have run marathons, ultra-marathons, and all-day adventure races. The only time I ever felt like I was going to puke after a race was after running a 5K.

Running a 5K race required extreme effort for a condensed period, and I discovered that this was definitely *not* my forte! A critic might judge me for being an inefficient runner or incapable of running a fast 5K, but I could run fifty miles. That might be something *they* were never able to do. Different journeys, neither one wrong. Bill Rodgers was a fantastic American marathoner who won the illustrious Boston Marathon four times. He could run 26.2 miles in just over two hours and did so numerous times. This elite athlete often expressed his respect for the back-of-the-packers. He is quoted as saying, "I can't even imagine what it's like to run for five or six hours." Different journeys. Neither one is wrong and neither one is the "easy" way out.

Another example is getting a tattoo. If you've never had a tattoo, there are usually two stages. The first stage is the outlining, and it usually involves the use of small number of needles that go deeper into the skin, because the outline needs to be darker. The second stage is the shading and/or colouring. This stage usually involves the use of a line of four to six finer needles, but they don't puncture the skin as deeply as the outlining needles. The outlining can be pretty intense, but in relation to the time it takes to complete the whole piece, the duration of the outlining portion is usually fairly short. The shading can take many more hours, depending on the size of the piece, and this phase is what can leave many people calling for a break. Is the outlining easier? Some would say yes, and others would say they have a higher tolerance for the finer shading needles. Neither one is "right."

We probably all have those friends who appear to have an easy life. They're bright, beautiful, their parents have money, they couldn't lose at the casino if they tried... Even if you are one of these people, there's probably someone you know who appears to have it better. We sometimes envy these friends, but the truth is that we, as humans, tend to learn much more from making mistakes than we do from doing things right. In addition, it can be difficult to detach ourselves from an addiction to material things when we "have it easy." It can often take many years of buying things like a better car, a bigger house, and more expensive clothes, before we discover that those things don't actually make us happy. We also talked about stress in Lesson 2 and how it can help us grow. The easy path doesn't necessarily provide that stress, and it may take longer to learn things that those of us who endure some hardships learn very quickly.

Sometimes, the Universe will actually try and hand you situations that will expand your horizons by forcing you out of your comfort zone, which helps you grow. Often times, the skills you acquire by experiencing these situations, will be crucial at a later point in your life. If you're a rock-jumping, outlining, human rocket, you may encounter a situation in your life that requires you to build your endurance skills. If you have become expert at conserving your energy to feed your endurance, you may be offered opportunities that offer big rewards, but only if you go "all-in" and figure out how to sprint.

In the creek, the beautiful "babbling brook" sounds are only made as the water runs over the rocks on the shallow part of the creek bed. The deeper, faster moving water is usually pretty quiet, which is not what most people love about a small stream or creek. I guess the biggest take-away from all of this is don't criticize (yourself or others), and don't compare. Your experiences are equipping you with the exact tools you will need for your life. Stepping into someone else's experience (as you perceive it) might equip you with tools you couldn't use. As we expand on the recurring theme of mutual respect from last lesson, you need to respect your own journey too. Sometimes we're hard on ourselves, which can lead to criticism instead of appreciation. That's not what we need!

Your perception of what's happening around you is limited, if not completely wrong. I know this sounds harsh, but think about how much we hear compared to what a dog can hear. Think about how little of the light spectrum the human eye can see (less than 1 percent). Our brains will also discard information received by the eyes, if that information isn't considered to be pertinent to the task at hand. This phenomenon is demonstrated by the popular video that appeared on Facebook some time back, in which people are asked to count passes of a basketball between people dressed in white moving around in a circle. The majority of viewers are so focused on counting passes between the moving people, they don't notice a person dressed in a black gorilla suit walking right through the group of people passing the basketball.

Many times, our perception of what's happening in our own lives can be a little foggy, never mind what's happening in someone else's! Who hasn't been condemned to an extra-long wait because we picked the "wrong line" at the grocery store? Our perceptions can mislead us and send us off to what looks like a more direct route to our goal. Then you find out that the woman in front of you at the checkout has thirty-two coupons and is price matching everything else in her cart. You look longingly over at the next line, the one you didn't take because there were four people in it, and think, *I probably would have been in my car by now if I'd chosen that line...*

Looks can be deceiving! Do you have things in your life that you wish you had done differently? Our present can be destroyed by our past in seconds. Our regrets can suck the life out of us. In his book, *The Four Agreements,* Don Miguel Ruiz tells us to "always do our best" because if you are always doing your best, you can't second guess yourself when you revisit past events. Often, when we have regrets about things that didn't go well in our lives, we compare the choices we made to what we felt were our other options. Only thing is that we use the best possible outcome of our imagined option to compare with something that did not go well in our reality. Kind of an unfair comparison, right? You didn't know then what you know now. Give yourself the understanding that you try to give others, and realize that you have gained invaluable experience.

The many paths that the creek takes each have their own value. Often the bank-hugging, shallow water going over the little rocks gets to see more of its surroundings. If the point of your life is to enjoy the journey and not just worry about the destination, this path has its merits. If you came to this life with a plan, and you have a specific agenda, maybe the more direct route is a better fit for you. There's no one right way to be water in the creek, and all the different paths offer different experiences. The path that looks easier might not be faster, so the best approach is to find happiness where you are. We'll all have some great stories to share when we get to the lake!

THE JOURNAL:

Pick three regrets and head to your journal. Mentally go through your three regrets and what you wish you had done. Walk through the path you didn't choose and think about what could have gone wrong if everything didn't go right. Write down a few things that you learned from taking the path you did choose. Appreciate those lessons and congratulate yourself for growing from that experience. Be gentle with your past self. Remember, you didn't know then what you know now. Be happy where you are. This path is perfect for you.

LESSON 6:

THERE MAY BE A BIG ROCK IN YOUR PATH THAT LOOKS IMPASSABLE, OR AT LEAST LIKE IT MAY SLOW YOU DOWN.

IN NATURE, OBSTACLES LIKE THESE CAN, IN FACT, SPEED UP YOUR PROGRESS USING A PHENOMENON KNOWN AS THE VENTURI EFFECT.

I think many of us have been here: Life is good, things are ticking merrily along, and then... BAM!!! A huge boulder is dropped down in front of us! An event like this can stop you in your tracks and leave you asking yourself, "Why me?" or "Why did this have to happen right now, when things were going along really well? What do I do now?"

We've all heard many sentiments about making lemonade out of life's lemons, but what does this mean in the practical sense? How am I supposed to make lemonade out of a house fire, getting laid off or the death of a loved one? Events like these require huge adjustments and time to grieve. You do not have to apologize for the time it takes you to do those things. You are absolutely allowed time to catch your breath. You are absolutely allowed to go through the stages of grief and feel devastated. What you are not allowed to do is shore up supplies, batten down the hatches and live there.

This process (and it is a process, not a new, stagnant way of life), this pain, suffering, and period of massive adjustment will speed your learning. If you can manage to accept the pain and not resent it, go through the suffering and try not to avoid it, the experience will hasten your enlightenment and learning in this life. This can be impossible to see when you're in your darkest times. Give yourself time to know and have faith that you will know. The faster you accept, the faster you get past it. Understanding helps a lot in this regard, so here's how it works:

There is a phenomenon in physics called the Venturi Effect, and it is named for Gianni Battista Venturi (1746- 1802). Venturi was an Italian physicist who discovered that when a fluid, (like water in a creek!), is forced through a tube that decreases in diameter, the pressure that the fluid exerts on the tube decreases, while the velocity of the fluid through the tube increases. In plain English, this means that if you, as a water droplet, are forced between a rock and a hard place, you and all your fellow water droplets have no choice but to speed up. I find a great deal of comfort in this idea when I'm going through a rough time. I like that this concept addresses the now, as opposed to so many well-known sayings that may be true but focus on the future. Ideas like "this too will pass" and "it's always darkest before the dawn" are certainly true, but when? And more to the point, what do I do in the meantime?

Our society is notorious for the lengths to which it is willing to go to seek convenience and comfort. We build extravagant homes and luxurious cars, we have drive-through just about everything, and we can have anything from shampoo to a piano delivered to our front door by Amazon. We seek the same level of comfort in our life experiences. The thing is that growth is not comfortable. That's why we have growing *pains!* A life-altering trauma is *not* comfortable. It's not supposed to be, and comfort isn't the ultimate achievement.

Many of the people who are trying to cheer you up during your down times are trying to relieve your pain, or at least distract you from it, to make themselves feel more comfortable. Some people might avoid you all together. We are all connected, and it's natural for your pain to be uncomfortable for the people around you who care about you. A true friend, who realizes that your pain is part of your recovery, will sit with you in your pain in spite of their own discomfort. Don't get me wrong, we all need a good laugh and often! Not being able to laugh was one of the things I missed the most after my ex-husband left me.

We also need a select few people who will stand by us while we hurt. Accepting the pain is the only way to get through it. You have to sit with your emotions and really *feel* them, as it's only then that you can let them go. It's incredibly hard and the only way to grow. These days our society would like us to believe that a successful life is a comfortable, stress-free life, and this just breeds unrealistic expectations and disappointment. As discussed in the last lesson, taking the "easy" route can also take longer.

We have talked about stress and its role in Lesson 2, and this is a prime example of how stress can speed up our growth if we can acknowledge, accept, and make a change. There are very few among us who will choose to grow when they are comfortable. We generally wait until we don't feel we have a choice. It will take some time before you can look back at your trauma as a blessing, and if you keep trying to avoid working through the pain, you may never see it that way. We must not get comfortable with avoidance. Think more along the lines of "no pain, no gain."

Try to remember that the times of greatest trauma offer the greatest opportunities to speed up your growth. Quite often, it is a traumatic event that forces us to rethink our tolerance, endurance or mild dissatisfaction associated with living an ordinary life. If we weren't shaken up a bit, we might never choose to move. A boulder dropped in the middle of the creek will speed the progress of the water droplets down the creek bed, through the phenomenon known as the Venturi Effect.

THE JOURNAL:

Write down a painful situation in your life. Any present dilemma or past situation that still haunts you will work as an example. Write about it. Write everything you feel about it. This is between you and the Universe, so don't hold back and don't sugar-coat it. Write down every feeling: the hurt, the fears, the regrets, the betrayal, the inability to forgive, the pain you still feel... EVERYTHING!

Don't avoid this. It's really hard, but do it anyway. Have some tissues handy. Write until your hand gets sore. Write until you're really done. Don't put a time limit on it. When you think that you have really written down everything that you feel, rip the page out of your journal. Get a lighter or a match, take the page outside, crumple it up, and set it on fire. Put the page down before it burns you! As it's burning, say, "I am releasing my suffering and pain related to this event or situation."

I had a difficult time with this part immediately after my breakup, because I felt like if I healed, it meant I was giving up on my husband. What I realized is that letting go is not giving up. Healing can also be difficult if you've gotten a lot of attention from being wounded. The most well-meaning friends can forget that you need their support to continue even when you're getting stronger. As a result, there can be a significant temptation to keep the wound open, but you can't go forward if you're still turned around, hanging on to the past. Let it go.

Now, I want you to think of one good thing in your life—one happy thought that makes you smile when you think it, and then go ahead and think it. It could be a family member, a friend, a child or grandchild, a funny joke, a happy memory or anything else that makes you smile. Hold that feeling in your thoughts until your heart starts to lighten a little. Make a conscious effort to smile (don't wait for the feeling to produce the smile), because it's almost impossible to feel bad if your face is smiling. Tell yourself that this is how you want to feel now. It won't last forever, but it will last longer each time you practice thinking it, so try to think a happy thought several times throughout the day. You can even set an alarm if you have to. If you can't think of one good thought, remember that you are loved. If you think no one loves you, you're wrong. I love you.

LESSON 7:

SOMETIMES YOU CAN GET CAUGHT UP IN A WHIRLPOOL, GOING AROUND AND AROUND, UNABLE TO GET AWAY FROM THAT CIRCULAR CURRENT.

IN INSTANCES LIKE THESE, A FLOOD, OR SOMETHING LIKE IT, CAN BE JUST WHAT YOU NEED TO FORCE YOU OUT OF THAT PATTERN.

Because the shoreline of almost every creek is anything but smooth, there are always places where the water will get caught in circular pools. It can often seem like the water caught up in this whirlpool pattern might go around in a circle forever, unless something drastic happens to break up that flow. The same is true in our lives.

    I said in Lesson 6 that sometimes your life will be ticking merrily along, and BAM!!, something major happens. Well, life may be going along at a certain comfortable pace and in the right general direction, but it may also be going in circles and we just don't notice. I remember a few years ago, I went on a bit of a cleaning spree. I have kept journals on and off for years, and while on my de-cluttering binge, I came across a journal I had written quite a few years prior. Of course, I had to flip through a few entries to see what had been going on in my life all those years earlier.

As I read through more and more entries, my stomach plummeted towards my feet. To my absolute horror, I discovered my complaints were almost all the same, my relationship concerns were almost all the same, my spiritual struggles were the same, and my dissatisfaction with my job was—you guessed it—the same. I was devastated!! I have sought after personal growth and spiritual enlightenment, with varying degrees of dedication, for decades! This was a brutal slap in the face! I suddenly felt that I hadn't changed or grown at all! It was like all those years meant nothing, because I hadn't learned a thing!

We, as humans, fall into some sort of whirlpool fairly often. Our lives, our planet and the cosmos, all have cyclical tendencies. There can be some comfort knowing the sun will rise tomorrow, spring will return after a long, hard winter, and that Friday is just a few days off when we head into the office on a Monday morning. Sometimes though, we give those tendencies more purchase than they're meant to have. We're in orbit, thinking that we just want to reach escape velocity, but we get scared the minute we get close, because that might change everything. Then we get upset or depressed, because nothing in our life changes.

Every once in awhile, the Universe is kind enough to bump us out of the whirlpool. The first "bump" or two are usually relatively gentle. If we don't pay attention, things can get a little more "in your face." My ex-husband and I actually split up once about eight years before his affair. We were separated for nine months but still in frequent contact. I couldn't cut the ties, and he didn't find anything he thought was better, so we got back together.

I didn't pay attention to the bump, and the next message from the Universe left me no option but to do what was best for me. No matter how painful our break-up was (it certainly felt like a kick in the gut!), it was the only option if I truly wanted to grow and be free. Now I realize that our break-up had to happen the way it did or I would have blindly kept trying, trapped in the circular motion of the whirlpool.

We can avoid this severe type of message if, when we feel the "bump", we stop asking how on earth we're going to keep doing "A" under these new circumstances, and start asking if we should keep trying to do "A" at all. These days, western society seems to have a more-is-better way of viewing life, which promotes a perfection-or-bust sort of mentality. What this looks like, in a practical sense, is something like this...

You want to lose some weight before bathing-suit season hits, so you start going to the gym and doing cardio three times a week. Great! You lose the first ten pounds and then hit a plateau. You end up in the plateau for a couple weeks, and then one of two things will happen: 1) You give up. "Why bother? It's not working! Maybe I'm just at the age where I can't lose weight anymore; after all, ten pounds is pretty good." 2) You start doing more, harder, faster. "Maybe I should start going to the gym five days a week. Maybe I could do two classes on Saturdays. Maybe I should start going to spin classes too."

Without the guidance of a personal trainer, very few people think to ask themselves if they should be doing cardio in the first place. They think, *But I've always done cardio to lose weight!*

Maybe it's time to shake things up a bit and try something completely different. The results may surprise you! I'm sure many of us are familiar with Einstein's definition of insanity, which states that insanity is doing the same thing over and over again and expecting different results. This circular thinking seems to be something many of us participate in. I asked myself, my friends and the Universe (for years), how I could make my relationship work, instead of asking if I should be trying to make it work at all.

The key here is to start asking yourself what else you can try rather than asking why what you continue to do isn't working. Our brain answers the questions we ask of it. This point is crucial! Your brain is a faithful servant (not who we really are) and will relentlessly seek answers. If you ask how you can make your workouts successful, your brain will find you some answers. If you ask why the gym isn't working for you, and why you're such a failure at losing weight, your brain will find those answers too.

So... if you're stuck in a cycle and don't want to wait for external forces to give you an unpleasant push, ask yourself the right questions. What can you do to make some small positive change today? Who can I go to for help or advice? What would I really like my life to look like? How can I make a living doing what I love? You get the idea. You don't have to wait for the flood or other major event to knock you on your ass before you decide to make a change. You can make the choice to change (remember choice involves action) before the change is forced upon you. Once your choice is made (action), karma kicks in with the reaction.

Sometimes, if you're lucky (and it doesn't always feel like luck), the Universe will hand you something to push you out of the vicious cycle— you just might not care for what the Universe considers a push. If you choose to stay stuck, or insist on doing more of the same, the Universe will continue to nudge you with increasing intensity until you listen. As I stated in Lesson 2, life floods rarely come out of the blue. Most people, myself included, will admit that they had been nudged towards change repeatedly before a flood, but they didn't pay attention, or they were scared, or change seemed too inconvenient.

If you do end up with a flood or a push, try and see it for what it is (I know, it's difficult!) and practice gratitude. Practice is the operative word in this case. You don't have to be perfect at it. Just try for glimpses of gratitude as opposed to settling into self-pity, bitterness and defeat. A habit of complaining and asking why this happened to you can be a cycle in itself. You are allowed to feel down when something happens that you perceive as negative. You just can't stay there. If you want something different, or less of the same, *do* something different or less of the same. Gratitude for the good things in your life is crucial for growth, whereas resignation and complacency just help you stay circling.

THE JOURNAL:

I often ask myself, "If money were no object, what would I be doing that I'm not doing now?"

Write down a few things, or even one big thing, that you would do that you're not doing now. "I've always wanted to _____." It's called finding your passion and setting your intention. Particularly if you've had a recent event that has pushed you out of the whirlpool, it helps to set your intention on the positive. This way, you look forward and don't get stuck in another whirlpool of negativity. Even if you haven't had a flood, you're probably reading this book because you're dissatisfied with at least some aspect of your life, and setting an intention will point you in the right direction as you make choices to change.

If you listen while you're writing this down, your ego self probably won't waste any time coming up with a whole list of reasons why this thing will never happen. "I'm too old, too fat, too broke, too whatever..." Many people feel their ego selves are just being realistic, but in truth, our egos can be assholes, and we tend to listen to that voice far more often than we should. Your spirit is the voice that wants you to shine. Your ego is the voice that wants you to shrivel. We certainly listen to ego's negativity more than we listen to our spirit's positive thoughts.

So, ignore the voice of your ego, and tell it that this is your time to spend with the real you—the you who is the dreamer of dreams and the believer in possibilities. Then look at what you would really love to do that you're not doing now. Write down some small steps that might move you just a teensy bit closer to being able to do that thing.

Have you always wanted to write a book? Well, journaling is a great place to start! Have you always wanted to run a marathon? There are reasonably priced learn-to-run clinics all over the world that will help new or non-runners get started without pushing too hard or injuring themselves. Have you always wanted to fly? Most flight schools have an intro-flight program, so people can see if they really like it without spending a ton of money. Have you always wanted to play a musical instrument? Many music stores will rent out instruments, and you can find a myriad of how-to videos online. Follow your bliss. The first steps can be uncomfortable, as you venture out of your well-worn routine, but keep going and you will start to align with your authentic self. This alignment will have you leaving all thoughts of that comfortable rut far behind in no time!

What can you do today? Or first thing tomorrow morning? Write a short story in your journal? Go for a walk with a couple of short running breaks thrown in? Call the flight school? Check out the website of a local music store?

Start with a step that's not monumental right now. Baby steps are where to start, so you don't get intimidated. Do something different to get something different! Then take a couple more, small steps, and watch the momentum kick in! As it builds, it will help you on your way out of the whirlpool and back down the creek. As you make positive choices, the Universe will respond positively, and oh boy, does that feel awesome!!!

LESSON 8:

SOMETIMES THE CREEK CAN GET PRETTY DRY,
AND YOU JUST HAVE TO WAIT IT OUT.

A RESPITE DOES NOT HAVE TO BECOME A RUT.

MOST TIMES, WITH PATIENCE AND A LITTLE RAIN,
YOU WILL GET STARTED ON YOUR JOURNEY AGAIN.

A few years ago, we had a very dry winter without much snow. That made winter pretty tolerable for those of us who don't ski, and like our family, don't own a snow-blower. It wasn't so good for the farmers or their crops. That winter was followed by an unusually dry spring and summer. Our creek looked (and smelled!) more like a string of random stagnant mud puddles than a flowing body of water. I couldn't help but notice, during my creek-side walks, that the puddles that were left were teeming with life: tadpoles, minnows, toads, etc.

The dry weather was not what all these different life forms would have preferred, I'm sure, but there in the puddles were so many examples of species that chose to ride out the dry weather. They continued their lives in the puddles, patiently waiting for the rain to come and for the creek to flow again.

Every single one of us has points in our lives where we're up to our necks in a foul-smelling puddle of creek water. These are difficult times, to be sure. We don't know when, or even if, the rain will come. Sometimes, it's hard to hang on to a small shred of hope when these times occur. Patience is crucial but sometimes difficult to cultivate. Dry spells like these can be opportunities to hone your skills. Like anything else, your proficiency will improve with practice, and your environment will change with your attitude.

If you can convince yourself to look at this situation as an opportunity rather than an oppression, everything inside you will change. As an inevitable consequence, everything outside you will change as well. So, check in on your friends in the other mud puddles to see how they're making out, and practice patience. Ask your brain what you can do to make the most out of your current situation, and practice patience. Sometimes things have to happen in the time it takes them to happen, and no amount of blustering, fussing or complaining will change that. Like the fermentation of wine or kombucha, you can help things along a bit, but you can't rush Mother Nature past a certain point. Practice patience.

Another option (and a very popular one, at that) is worrying. Recent scientific evidence has proven that if you worry, you die, and if you don't worry, you die anyway, so why worry? Well, the answer is a mistaken concept of what worry accomplishes. This misconception has become all too common in our society. People are confusing the concept of worry with the idea of planning. There is also a sense of obligation around worry as an expression of love. Worry is being confused with positive concepts in both these cases, so let's talk about them.

I'm a planner. I find comfort in the idea of having a plan in place. I'm not usually married to the plan exactly as I plan it, but I like the feeling of security that comes with planning certain things in life. I have always thought that, even if things didn't go exactly according to plan (do they ever?), at the very least, they should probably go in a similar direction on a similar schedule. We might get where we're going a bit later than planned, or we might get somewhere close to where we were planning on going when we thought we would. It's a kind of "shoot for the moon and you'll end up among the stars" approach.

Planning, provided it doesn't become an obsession, can go a long way in keeping us focused on our goals. Worry does not do that. Read that again. Worry does *not* do that. Worry doesn't help keep you focused; in fact, it's a distraction. It is not beneficial or constructive. Many people feel like they have to worry, because it will help somehow. They feel like something terrible might happen if they don't wait up, wringing their hands and fearing the worst. This is not planning. If you believe, as I do, that you get what you give and that our thoughts create our reality, what are you putting out to the Universe by imagining all sorts of horrible scenarios in your mind? At best? Nothing. At worst? You'll create your worst fears. Are you really doing your kids, husband, girlfriend, etc. any good? Your worrying won't help them, it certainly won't help you, and you're putting out some pretty negative vibes. Worry will limit what you do and rob you of any enjoyment while you're doing it. Planning will offer security and confidence, because you have a game plan in place if something unexpected happens.

The other misconception is that, if you don't worry, it means you don't care. People often ask me, "So, what am I supposed to do when my daughter's out on a first date? Go to bed?" In a word, yes! Get some sleep! Turn your ringer up, set an alarm for her curfew time, and get some sleep. If something terrible is going to happen, you'll be rested enough to deal with it with a clear head, and you won't have to feel guilty about sending negative vibes out to the Universe. If you want your daughter to feel like you care about her, wake up when she comes home and talk to her about her date. Share her excitement and practice some gratitude around the fact that she's growing up and experiencing the happy events that come with maturing. Practicing gratitude will help you share her joy and feel some of your own.

When the creek bed is so dry that only mud puddles remain, a rain shower is a welcomed, joyful occasion. While you wait for that, try to find positive options so you're not left with the negative ones. Losing your job can be awful, but maybe that will give you time to check in on friends, make nice dinners for your family, or go to the gym. You can also practice being still. Stillness has benefits that are only revealed with time and silence.

Worrying whether the rain will come will not speed its arrival. Practicing patience, gratitude and joy in the moment, will not only help you live in the present, instead of the past or the future, but it will also exercise those muscles for future use.

THE JOURNAL:

One of our society's biggest current issues is mental health. Anxiety and depression are rampant! Both of these conditions can be helped immensely by becoming present. There are so many books, articles and videos out there right now about mindfulness because it's a skill we have lost touch with. Take a deep breath and be right here, right now. It's often been said that anxiety stems from worrying about your future, while depression stems from an attachment to events in your past. Being present can help with both of these situations.

Write down what you're afraid of. If you come up with less than five things, keep asking yourself. I recently participated in a "goddess" workshop. One of the exercises involved us partnering up with another goddess. For five minutes, we looked into one another's eyes. One goddess was instructed to ask her partner what she was afraid of. The other goddess answered, and then the first goddess repeated the question: "What are you afraid of?" The partner would answer again with a different fear, and then the first goddess would ask again, "What are you afraid of?"

The answers quickly went from the superficial to the deep and dark, like peeling an onion. In just five minutes, women were addressing fears they had kept buried for years, in some cases. Do this in your journal. Keep asking for five minutes. You can burn this page when you're finished and release those fears to the Universe, if you feel comfortable doing so.

After you have finished the fear list, start a new list of things you're grateful for. Commit to adding three new things every day. I know everyone's talking about gratitude these days, and there's no better way to keep yourself all about "right now." Practicing gratitude will also make it much easier to experience joy. If you meditate, start and end your meditations with gratitude. If you don't meditate yet, lay in bed for a minute when you wake up in the morning (if you don't have to pee like a racehorse!), smile, and think about the three things in your life that you're grateful for right now. Starting your day with this new attitude of gratitude will cause a shift in the direction of your whole day. Gratitude attracts more stuff to be grateful for. Worry attracts more stuff to worry about. Decide where you want to direct your attention, and choose to focus your energy on the positive. You can use this time for good. It is your decision, and you have the power to choose gratitude over fear, while you practice patience and wait for some rain in your mud puddle.

LESSON 9:

SOMETIMES YOUR JOURNEY MAY CHANGE DIRECTION, AND WHERE YOU THOUGHT YOU WANTED TO END UP CAN CHANGE AS WELL.

YOU CAN CHANGE YOUR GOALS, AS LONG AS YOU DON'T GIVE UP ON HAVING THEM ALL TOGETHER.

Like the water droplets in the creek, many of us rush toward common goals. So many people seek "success" as measured by big houses, big incomes, big titles, nice cars, and other material indications of having "arrived." For the water droplets in Forty Mile Creek, the common goal is Lake Ontario. What I have noticed, after watching the creek over the last decade, is that not all the water droplets end up in the lake. Some of the water droplets evaporate, some feed the willows and vegetation along the creek banks, some feed the birds and wildlife that call the area home, and I think that some of us also opt for different goals.

I've tried many different jobs and careers in my lifetime. I've also owned a couple of my own businesses. There may be one or two vocations that I feel I "failed" at, but each has contributed to my library of life experience.

I've also been fortunate enough to have lived in several different countries, and the plan I had for my life has changed more times than I can count. When people said, "You never know until you try", I took it as a personal challenge and tried a LOT of different things. My point is that goals can change drastically as you go through your life, without abandoning the idea of having goals all together.

The water that evaporates, the water that feeds the flora and fauna, and the water that saturates the creek bed is all as important as the water that flows into the lake, and vice versa. *And vice versa.* There has been a common trend of late to have some contempt for those of us who strive for conventional success as described earlier. There can be some critical judgement implied, as some of us try to embark on a more minimalist path or live according to a more spiritual set of values. We are all on this plane to experience and to learn. We cannot judge the path anyone else chooses to make their way through the Universe.

This acceptance without critical judgement is yet another example of true liberalism. I feel compelled, at this point in my experience, to seek other forms of success than the material things previously mentioned. That's my path. The corporate world doesn't interest me at all, and as a result, I have been largely unable to accomplish much in that forum. Will I criticize those who are more adept at navigating that world than I? My choice of path doesn't make me more or less evolved than anyone else; it just makes me different. I certainly use and appreciate many technological and scientific advances produced by the world corporate, so I can't very well criticize those who have provided me with those advances.

Most of us have the same goals of accomplishment, happiness and satisfaction; we just go about getting there in different ways. Like every other water droplet in the creek, I am on my own path, and I realize that without those other paths, mine might not exist. That being said, if my path exists on the grounds of exploiting you and your path, it's probably not a good thing. Still, in the end, it's not for me to judge. Relationships run on complicated paradigms and dynamics. As we talked about in Lesson 4, both the users and usees are responsible in cases of exploitation, as martyrs create persecutors. The point of this lesson is that you are free to change your mind, your goals or your direction, whenever you want. If you have obligations, fulfill them and then start your new path. Give two-week's notice at your job and then start your new career. Finish out your season with the team you joined and then sign up for a pottery class. Do what you need to do, so you can start doing what you want to do.

If people are trying to make you feel guilty about changing direction, or if you are like me and do that to yourself, the *Ho'oponopono* is a great tool. My energy healer introduced me to this Hawai'ian healing process. It is very powerful as a meditation or visualization to work toward forgiveness. The process can address the forgiveness you're asking for or struggling to offer. You begin by picturing the other person in question standing in front of you. Picture them in as much detail as you can. If you're really angry, I sometimes find picturing them as a child helpful. Then you look them in the eyes while you say each of the following four steps. The explanation of each step follows.

I love you
I'm sorry
I forgive you
Thank you

I love you: Kind of self-explanatory but challenging. It doesn't have to mean I like you. It doesn't have to mean that we like the same things. It doesn't even have to mean that I can relate to your chosen path. It means I want what's best for you, I want to see you shine, and I will never wish any ill on you. We are drops from the same creek.

I'm sorry: Wait! What? I'm supposed to be sorry??? This can be tough to digest if you're the one who's angry, but it's about responsibility. We all pick our own journeys and our own lessons. Even if I don't realize yet what lessons I'm working on, I'm sorry that I needed you to play this role in my life (it was probably hard for you too!), so that I could learn those lessons. Like I said before, no one really wants to be a jerk, but if a jerk is what I needed so I could learn what I had to learn from a given situation, I'm sorry that task fell on you.

I forgive you: If you feel that your anger is justified, this can also be a tough one. I found it helpful to remember that my forgiveness was not about "letting someone else off the hook", it was about not letting past events eat up my present and my future. It's also about realizing that this person needed to play this role in my life, not only for me, but also so they could learn their own lessons. Therefore, you're no different from me, and I forgive you.

Thank you: I am grateful that you are/were in my life in this capacity, because you helped me grow and learn the lessons I needed to learn to keep moving forward.

We are all here to experience life, and while our goals may be different, we all have that in common. Keep following your path no matter how many turns or detours you end up taking. Goals are like clothes; as you grow, they may no longer fit. That doesn't mean you start running around naked; it just means you get better-fitting clothes! The turns and redirections you take as a result of learning and growing are good changes, so embrace them. The changes your fellow water droplets make as a result of their learning and growing are also good changes, and not judgement of you. It's important to realize that people will move into and out of your life, because they have different directions and rates of growth. In just the same way, you will move into and out of other people's lives as a result of your different rates of growth and directions. This is what we're meant to do, so if you need to change direction, *Ho'opono pono* the people that change will affect, and move on. If someone in your life has changed their direction, *Ho'opono pono* them, and let them move on. Work on understanding that some people in your life may feel hurt as a result of you trying to make positive changes. You may also feel hurt as a result of someone in your life trying to make positive changes. It doesn't mean either of you should stop trying to grow. It doesn't mean either of you is a bad person. It doesn't mean either of you is wrong. There is no one right way to be water in the creek.

THE JOURNAL:

Well, this isn't really a journal exercise, but it's a goodie anyway. Think about someone in your life who has hurt you or angered you, or someone you feel you may have hurt. Close your eyes and picture them with as much detail as you can. Spend some time on this, so you can really see them standing in front of you, and then say the *Ho'opono pono* out loud to them.

This will be really hard, I know. The first time I tried to do this picturing my mom, I almost threw up. It was much the same when I first started trying to do it while picturing my ex-husband. It's hard and incredibly beneficial, so do it anyway.

You can do this every day, until it doesn't carry such pain with it. It's really hard, and it helps you heal. If you can be honest enough with yourself to shed a little light on your dark parts, and you realize you've been a victim, or a bully or hurtful, write about this. These behaviours usually come from a fear of being hurt that manifests as a desire to manipulate or control people around you. Now, equipped with this new insight, you can revisit Lesson 8 and rewrite a list of fears that may have come up with this exercise.

You can burn and release this list also. I offer this suggestion quite a bit, but burning a page after you've poured your heart out on it in writing, is very cathartic. After that, stand in front of a mirror and do the *Ho'opono pono* to your reflection. Seriously. You deserve your love, forgiveness and gratitude just as much as the next guy.

When you get comfortable doing this (and that may take a while—we're just not used to being good to ourselves this way), head back to your journal and write down five things you would like to accomplish in the next five weeks. Make them attainable so you can take action. If you continue coming from a place of "I've always wanted to _____" you will keep creating more of that same wanting to _____ but not doing _____. Just remember, choice involves action and only action creates reaction. Your goals can change, as long as you actually keep moving towards them.

Check back in with your list of things you want to do from Lesson 7. Don't be surprised if you don't want to do all of those things now. Incorporate some little goals from the things you do still want to do, and commit to take action. As we grow, our goals will evolve. It's a good thing!

LESSON 10:

MANY HAVE TRAVELLED THIS PATH BEFORE YOU. AVAIL YOURSELF OF THEIR WISDOM.

YOU DON'T HAVE TO FOLLOW THEIR PATH, BUT IF YOU DO, BE GRATEFUL THAT THEY HAVE SMOOTHED THE CREEK BED FOR YOU.

I was unsure of whether I should include this as a separate lesson from Lesson 3 or not, but I decided to include it on its own because having company (going through something together) and following (going through something others have been through before) offer different advantages. This lesson is helpful to avoid the common situation where history repeats itself.

I saw a post on Facebook the other day about the top thirty-seven regrets that people have when they get older. My immediate thought was *Thirty-seven???If that is just the top of the list, does that mean that most of us have more regrets than that? Yikes! That's way too much regret to live with!*

Anyway, not surprisingly, not listening to our parents enough was in the top ten. I found this a little misleading, because typically in modern western culture, we don't listen to our elders at all! Many societies have incredible respect for their elders and those of any age who possess special wisdom. Families and whole tribes will listen when the sacred ones speak, because their insight and stories are considered invaluable. Elders are revered and many with what we would consider mental illness, are treated as oracles or prophets. Children who demonstrate special gifts are considered intuitives.

Nowadays, in western society, we tend to tuck our elders, special children, mentally ill and socially disenfranchised away in different institutions and patronize them at best. We've all heard horror stories, but I think the majority of these homes and schools offer high-quality care. If someone in your life is beyond your capability of care or teaching, moving them into a loving environment where they can be provided for by experts in the field, is best for them and you. Imagine though, if we treated our elders, children and intuitives with the same reverence and inclusion that native cultures do.

In these cultures, geriatric diseases, mental illnesses and childhood trauma occur at a fraction of the rate they do in our "advanced" society, because everyone is treated with respect, acceptance and admiration. Indigenous cultures, living in accordance with the ways handed down over generations, realize that there is education here that extends beyond knowledge, and they listen. It's wisdom, and those imparting it feel heard and valued. Community members are not so arrogant or ignorant as to think that this is the first time throughout the ages that life has been this way.

They recognize, in that cyclical process that we talked about in Lesson 7, that there really isn't anything new under the sun. Have we ever had such easy access to technology in our history? Probably not, and definitely not in recent times. Do we think the introduction of industry was so different? Radio? Phones? TV? Relatively speaking, all these innovations were just as amazing and just as impactful. We think we're smarter than all of that now, don't we? "It's different now," we tell ourselves. "We're much more advanced."

But are we? The first trip to the moon in July of 1969 rocked the socks off the world. There have been many periods, in recent history, of huge advancements, and I'll bet many people who were adults during those periods would have some solid, hard-won advice based on their experience, if we would just listen. We are cycling back into an expanding collective consciousness that, until recently, was considered "crazy", but one that intuitives and indigenous cultures have recognized for centuries. They have wisdom to offer, if we just listen. Just because we have labelled someone as too old, too young or mentally ill, doesn't mean they don't have wisdom to offer.

Lesson 1 tells us that they (like us) are beautiful souls on the inside, if we just listen. Not listening is like having a leaky roof and not calling a roofer. We can always get together with some of our non-roofer friends and watch a YouTube video on DIY roof repair. After all, roofs are different now, technology is better than experience, and I'm not going to waste my time and money on some old-school, blue-collar labourer who's only been doing this as a specialty for like twenty years... I'm smarter and more technologically adept than that guy! Do you feel the same about your airline pilot? I've never landed a jet, but I rock at flight sims! I don't need to learn from an actual pilot in an actual plane, do I?

Give respect where respect is due, and listen. Defer to those with more experience. We, as a society, seem so reluctant to concede our limitations, as though admitting the fact that I don't know everything about everything is some sort of weakness. Worse yet, we inflict our insecurities on our children. Teachers are forbidden to criticize, because it might damage their student's egos. Parents can't say anything "bad" to their kids, because it means they're "bad" parents. Everyone gets a medal and we don't keep score, so no one has to lose and we don't have to deal with the discomfort of seeing our kids disappointed. As a result, the illusion is maintained and the egos are alive and thriving. Unfortunately, those egos aren't who we really are, or who we should strive to be.

Are we actually preparing our children for the real world? How can I figure out what I'm good at if no one will tell me what I'm bad at? How am I supposed to figure out where my gifts truly lie, when I don't know whether your compliments are heartfelt or arbitrary? Maybe you're just sugar coating it for me, because my guilt-ridden, over-protective, both-working-seventy-hours-a-week parents might complain about you if you don't. It has been proven that our "everyone gets a medal" approach is hugely damaging to our children, because the ones who don't deserve the medals know they're just getting a patronizing pat on the head, and the ones who do deserve the medals are resentful, because it belittles their achievements if everyone gets one. You know what's better? Telling our kids the truth.

I made the high-school girls basketball team when I was in grade nine. I was ecstatic! My parents were artistic, and athletic prowess was not something they valued or encouraged. Nonetheless, I was always desperate to be athletic, so this was a huge accomplishment in an area I loved. I saw a good five minutes of court time that whole first season, but I didn't care. I was on the team! The next year, I tried out again, of course. Well, there were a few good grade-nine ballers that had come up, so Mrs. Dykman, the coach, had to have "the talk" with me. I didn't make the team, and I was heartbroken. I was invited to stay on as an assistant manager, but it was humiliating.

I have to tell you that Mrs. Dykman was, and still is, one of my favourite teachers of all time. This woman, who handed me what was perhaps the biggest athletic disappointment of my life, liked me. She told me I was smart, quick witted and had a "going places" personality. I could actually believe her, because she was honest enough to cut me from the basketball team. You can't build that kind of trust without constructive criticism or when everyone gets a medal. We do our children a monumental disservice by not being honest with them, and ourselves a disservice by not respecting the experience and wisdom of those who have gone before. In addition, when we demonstrate respect for people's talents and accomplishments, they feel valued for what they're good at, and less concerned about what they're not good at. That puts the focus on the positive. It also removes feelings of inadequacy around not knowing everything about everything. What a great example and relief for our children!

We are never too old to learn or too young to teach. Self-esteem is built by successfully honing certain skills. This means being good at some things, as opposed to being less-than-average at everything. It means that trying something I'm not good at is more of a direction sign than a failure, and now I can move on and try something else. Self-realization and joy come from doing what we're good at, so figuring out where our talents lie is imperative to achieving true happiness. I wasn't good at basketball, and finding this out freed me up to continue searching for what I was good at. It must have been very difficult for Mrs. Dykman to tell me I didn't make the team, but I sure appreciated her honesty and her wisdom. She took the hard road to help me, which then begs the question: When everyone gets a medal, who are we actually trying to make it easier for? In my case, I was able to avail myself of some wisdom from someone I looked up to and respected, because I trusted her honesty, and because she had been down the creek before me.

THE JOURNAL:

Do you have people in your life who excel in areas that interest you? Do you know anyone who may have gone through something you're going through? Talk to them, but more importantly, listen to them. Ask questions and hear the answers. Listen to hear, not just to reply. You already know what you know; you don't know what *they* know. Treat them like the treasure chests of knowledge and wisdom they are, and watch what happens. They will bloom, and you will learn. Encourage your children to do the same. When they learn to listen and respect, it's an investment in your future as well! Talk to your children, their friends, your friends, co-workers and maybe your whacky aunt. If anyone says something you don't understand, ask them to explain. Write down what speaks to you. I guarantee this exercise will benefit both you and them. You get some tips and insights, and they get the joy of imparting some of their wisdom to an appreciative audience. In his 2018 Kelowna TEDxTalk, Dr Mark Holder informed us that the three words that can ensure happiness are, "Tell me more." Conversations like these spark feelings of self-worth, mutual respect and connectedness, and both parties end up feeling great!

LESSON 11:

EVERY DROP COUNTS. EVERY DROP CHANGES THE LAKE IT ENTERS, AND THE LAKE CHANGES EVERY DROP.

YOU CHANGE THE LIVES YOU TOUCH, AND THE PEOPLE YOU MEET CHANGE YOU THROUGH YOUR EXPERIENCE OF THEM. THEY ALL HELP YOU GROW AS YOU HELP THEM.

I guess this lesson is the most appropriate one in which to dive in to the concept of karma, or the idea that what you give out, you get back. There are many misconceptions about karma, the most prevalent being that karma has a subjective quality. Karma behaves more objectively, like Newton's third law of motion, which states, "Every action has an equal and opposite reaction." Choice is the action and karma is the reaction. Karma won't "punish" you for doing something wrong, it just reacts with the same energy as the initial action.

The creek handed over this lesson after quite a bit of rain had fallen, and the creek was high and running fast. The area of the creek bed that was covered by water was greater, and the increased speed meant that the water had momentum to pick up more sand and silt. There was also a lot more run-off from its tributaries, all feeding water into the creek.

So, say I'm a water droplet carrying six grains of sand, from a little feeder brook, into Forty Mile Creek. At the point where I enter the creek, there are other droplets that aren't carrying any grains of sand. According to the laws of nature, I share my grains of sand with one of my neighbouring droplets, and I end up carrying only three grains. Now my neighbour and I each have three grains. We go along and end up in the lake. I meet many other droplets who have no grains. According to the laws of nature, I give a grain to two of my neighbours, and now each of us has one grain. As I swirl around the lake, I come close to the bottom. I nudge the lakebed, and my grain jumps off, thanking me for the ride. I continue to swirl and end up back by the mouth of the creek, where I meet up with a water droplet who has two grains of different sand. According to the laws of nature, my fellow droplet gives me a grain. Now each of us has one grain. The point I'm making in this oversimplified version of what happens at a river or creek delta is that we are constantly affecting those around us, and in turn, they affect us.

There are three morals to take away from this story:

1. You are a completely unique collection of your experiences and your reactions to those experiences.

2. Be careful how you influence or affect those around you. One harsh word can change someone forever, and one kind word can do the same. Always be kind and do your best to make your creek a better place.

3. Be careful who you choose to surround yourself with, because they will change you whether you want them to or not. Pick good people who inspire you, care about you and help your growth. This way, any changes you experience as a result of their influence will probably be good also.

Sometimes it's difficult to feel like you matter when there are millions of people "like you" in this world. When you become a bit more comfortable demonstrating what makes you unique, it can get lonely, because you may find it more difficult to find others who you can relate to. In any case, if you give someone a piece of advice that they follow up on, or help someone get over a hump, it's easier to feel needed, useful and important.

When you're the first person to offer advice or the first bit of help that doesn't quite solve the problem, you can sometimes feel like you're not needed, useful, or important, because your influence isn't immediately obvious. If it takes three times for a person to hear an idea and then adopt it, the first, second, and third times the person hears the idea are all equally important. Even though the third person gets the satisfaction of seeing the results, he or she wouldn't have been the third person without the other two. You matter. The whole world would change a little if you weren't in it. The following quote by Martha Graham demonstrates this exact idea:

> *"There is a vitality, a life force, an energy, a quickening that is translated through you into action, and because there is only one you in all time, this expression is unique. And if you block it, it will never exist through any other medium, and it will be lost. The world will not have it. It is not your business to determine how good it is nor how valuable nor how it compares to other expressions. It is your business to keep it yours, clearly and directly, to keep the channel open. You do not even have to believe in yourself or your work. You have to keep yourself open and aware of the urges that motivate you. Keep the channel open…"*
>
> — Martha Graham

Another school of thought that has gathered some momentum in recent years states that what you think, the energy that you exude, as well as what you do and how you interact with the world, all change humanity a little, because we are all connected. Your views and behaviour can change the Universal Consciousness. This Consciousness is thought to pervade every living and non-living thing on this planet, which is why we are thought to all be connected.

Once again, the role of water in our world offers somewhat of an analogy. We are all mostly water so, just as the moon affects the tides, it also affects us. You add the spice that is uniquely you to the soup pot of humanity by your actions and your intentions. This idea is a little more abstract but still great motivation to always do our best, and great motivation to feel as important as we really are. I'll address this in a bit more depth in Lesson 12. The important thing to realize is that connection is not an option, your presence is required and your input is a necessary ingredient, even if you can't see that from where you're standing.

The main take away from this lesson is the importance of faith and detachment. Have faith in the necessity of your influence and let go of the outcome. Your role, what you're doing and thinking, is the only thing that's any of your business. Obviously, we make ourselves aware of our surroundings through our observations. What we want to strive for is a response rather than a reaction. A reaction is an immediate backlash, the operative part of that being "back." You get "back" at someone with your reaction.

Responding is more forward thinking. You take a breath, assess the situation, decide what you would like to see happen, and choose what action you wish to take to go forward. Then you do what you can or what you choose to do, and let it go. Have faith that your input is important, give it, let go of your attachment to the outcome, and move along. This is a great mindset, especially if you're afraid someone may not be happy about what you have to say or do.

When you're not attached to the outcome, it makes it easier to keep being your authentic self, because you're not worried about screwing something up, pissing someone off, or what they will do with the insight you provide. This is not an excuse to be mean or hurtful! You are not trying to control the outcome, but you are still trying to love the person. Exercise compassion but don't be a pushover. Make sure your only agenda is to do what you can to help, not enable and certainly not to hurt.

We all enjoy seeing someone we've helped succeed, but we can become pretty stagnant while we wait for that to happen. Someone further along your path who also needs your help may miss out, while you're hanging around either patting yourself on the back for someone else's accomplishments, or worse yet, fretting over why that person isn't doing amazing things since you helped them. Pat yourself on the back for helping. That is the extent of your role, and you did it. Have faith that it's enough and then let go. You change the droplets you touch, and they change you. Practice gratitude for all the times either opportunity has occurred in your own life.

THE JOURNAL:

Write down three or four experiences in your life that knocked you down a bit or lifted you up. Write down a few points about what each situation taught you. By recognizing these points and writing them down, you give your unique insight up to the Universal Consciousness and gain appreciation for what you've already learned. You not only identify and solidify the knowledge you gained for future use in your own life, you also gain some evidence to bolster your faith in the importance of outside influences in all our lives. Make a list of people who contributed to your wisdom (even if their role seemed negative at the time) and practice gratitude for them.

Spend some time thinking about how the insights you gained as a result of your experiences have contributed to making you who you are. You will be able to find value in experiences that may have been painful or difficult, as these situations generally contribute the most to our growth. You will also be able to look at what you can learn from good experiences, by figuring out what actions you might like to repeat.

The vast majority of people spend most of their lives trying to avoid potentially hurtful situations, so they don't continue to get hurt. Something painful happens, and we think, *Well! I'm never doing THAT again!* This isn't a bad thing. Learning from our mistakes is a crucial part of the human experience, but it can end up keeping us backward focused. People who describe themselves as feeling fulfilled, live their lives trying to create or repeat good experiences, i.e. forward focused. Think of it as pulling yourself towards what you want, instead of pushing yourself away from what you don't want. They are very different approaches and produce very different results. As humans, we tend not to think about what we can learn from "good" experiences when everything is golden. We just take credit for a job well done!

Take some time to figure out and appreciate what you've been contributing, even by your mere presence. Just by reading this book and working on self-improvement, you are contributing more positive energy to everyone around you. You're discovering your gifts. Try and detach yourself from your self-doubt and think about this from the perspective of the other people in your life. You will probably be surprised at just how valuable your unique contributions have been and will continue to be. Being grateful for the contributions of the other droplets in your life helps you, because it makes it easier to recognize the lessons your own experiences have equipped you with. You can then contribute your well-earned wisdom to the lives of the water droplets you touch.

LESSON 12:

YOU ARE A CRUCIAL PART OF YOUR ENVIRONMENT.

YOU ARE INEXTRICABLY INTERTWINED
WITH EVERYTHING AROUND YOU.

YOU MAY NOT BE TOUCHING THE CREEK BED,
BUT YOUR PRESENCE ALLOWS ANOTHER WATER
DROPLET TO TOUCH IT AND BE ABSORBED, WASH
AWAY A GRAIN OF SAND OR POLISH A STONE.

WHAT YOUR PRESENCE HAS HELPED THAT WATER
DROPLET TO ACCOMPLISH CHANGES ALL THE
WATER DROPLETS EXPERIENCE OF THE CREEK.

This lesson relates to the previous one by expanding on the idea that our actions as individuals affect other individuals, and as a result, the creek as a whole. In this lesson, we consider the idea that we are not only "all in this creek together" but dives in to the idea that we are actually all connected.

I'm sure most of us have heard of the Butterfly Effect, which states that if a butterfly flaps its wings at precisely the right moment in New Mexico, that action and its cascade of reactions over time could eventually produce a hurricane in China. This can be used as a loose representation of the idea that we are all connected through a Universal Consciousness.

We are all stardust. It's a well-known fact that the molecules in our Universe have been floating around since the Big Bang. The carbon, hydrogen, and oxygen atoms that make up your body may well have been part of a star that exploded millions of years ago, or part of a meteor that crashed into earth before mankind developed. Who knows what our molecules will become part of after we die? The point is that we're all made of the same stuff physically, and we're also all connected through a Universal Consciousness mentally and spiritually.

There was a movie released in 2000 called *Pay It Forward,* based on a novel of the same name by Catherine Ryan Hyde. The movie received mixed reviews from critics, but the concept's popularity took off. Loosely, the premise is that I do something nice for you (or better yet, for a couple of yous) and in turn, you do something nice for someone else (or better yet, a couple of someone elses). Before you know it, there's a whole whack of people being good to one another.

What a great idea! It's a real-life example of practicing faith and detachment. You do something nice for someone, and in so doing, you have faith that they will appreciate your actions and "pay it forward". You detach from the need to follow up or fret about whether they actually do it or not. You do what you feel is right, and then you let it go. It works because we're all connected. Unfortunately, it works if we're at war or do something crummy as well but, for the purpose of this lesson, we'll focus more on the positive. So, all that's left for us to do is make a choice about how we're going to treat our connections to those around us.

I'm sure we've all known people who, against all odds, rise to a challenge or really shine when given some responsibility. I'm sure we've also all known people who feel the connection I speak of as pressure and as a result, they self-sabotage, so others will stop depending on them. Some people seem to take on everybody's problems and try to help, while some have "commitment issues," because they would like to be free of any connection.

The first group feels the connection and chooses to do what they can to assist their tribe. The second group seems selfish or self-absorbed, and I think this behaviour stems from some confusion about what their choice actually is.

The choice is not whether or not to be connected. The fact is you are. This is non-negotiable. The study of quantum physics now confirms this with the discovery of the Higg's Field, a field which infiltrates all space, time, atoms and particles. You are connected. The only choice you have is how you are going to treat the connections you have. I have found that many problems and stresses arise when there is a perception of more than one option. Again, this is about being careful with the questions you ask yourself. A good example of this phenomenon is marriage. The statistics are well known when we compare marriages say, fifty years ago, with marriages today. Some say only about half of the North American couples married today are likely to stay married to the same person (although the divorce rate has actually declined in recent years).

There have been all sorts of theories proposed as to why this is, so let me add mine to the mix! I think marriages today have such a dismal chance of success because, at least in part, we are confused about what our choices are. This leads us to ask the wrong questions. We ask *if* we can make our relationships work rather than *how* we can make them work. We ask if we made a mistake in our choice of commitment rather than asking if we're mistaken about our level of dedication to that commitment. Whatever question we ask, our brains will find an answer for. If there are two perceived options (yes or no), to the first part of each question, then our brains have a fifty-fifty chance of arriving at either of those answers. It will labour to decide which one is right. When the first parts of these questions are the focus, our brains never get to the second part of each question. This approach prevents our brains from discovering the many answers available to help improve our situation. Even if you decide to stay in your relationship, your brain doesn't get to discover ways to make things better because the question you asked it only requires a yes or no answer.

Now before anyone starts breaking out in a rash, I am certainly not suggesting that anyone stay in a dead-end, harmful, loveless or abusive relationship. The key word in the question "How can I make my relationship work?" is *work*. Not last, not endure, not survive, but *work*. An abusive relationship is not a relationship that's working. If it's broken, when you ask your brain the question "How do I make this work?" the answer may very well be "You can't", but you need to stop asking the yes-or-no question first, so you can get to this point. This is especially true if the other person isn't asking themselves the same question. In cases like this, the act of being good to yourself is just as crucial as being good to your partner. If we tie this back to the bully/victim scenario illustrated in Lesson 9, we can expand on that idea as it relates to this situation.

I touched on this concept in Lesson 9, and it involves not tolerating assholes. I can see many of you getting your backs up, fist pumping and enthusiastically telling the page/screen "Hell yeah! THAT'S what I'm talking about!" You may be a little disappointed with the lack of aggression that follows. I don't mean road rage, or telling off the annoying telemarketers who call in the middle of dinner, or sending your boss a nasty email. This is not an "Oh, yeah? Well I'll show you!" sort of proposal. It's about revisiting the concept of liberalism and not inflicting judgement. It's about calmly and clearly stating that you value yourself too much to tolerate that sort of behaviour and then walking away. No fisticuffs necessary.

What people don't realize is that, when someone is acting like an asshole and you give in, this confirms to that person that their behaviour is effective in achieving their desired outcome. You can calmly confront the person (whether they're acting like a jerk, or even a good person who has managed to wrong you in some way), or refuse to engage and walk away. If you give in, nothing changes. You feel walked on and the other person loses a little self-respect in the process. Let me repeat: victims and martyrs produce persecutors and tyrants. It's really a lose/lose situation, even though the other person may get what they think they wanted.

The responsibility falls equally on the shoulders of the walker and the walkee. This is not a popular sentiment in the present climate of blaming the persecutors, but the resistance to taking responsibility for our individual roles does not relieve us of responsibility for our actions. When we let people get away with bad behaviour because it's just "easier," we don't do them (or the other people in their lives) any favours. We may decide that lying down is the easiest choice, but other people in their lives may not be given that same choice before real damage is done. It will also encourage escalating behaviour between us and that person in our lives (if we want to continue our relationship with them), and things can easily get out of control. We later wonder (when things have proceeded to a critical point), "How did we get here?" The answer is often quite simple: one step at a time.

Think about spoiled children, outrageous celebrities, and bride-zillas, for example. I strongly believe that most bad behaviour is promoted by no one having the guts to say, "No, I refuse to accept that." Without resistance or rebuke, they continue to use that method of manipulation on more and more people, because it worked for them in the past. The more interactions they have where they prevail in this manner, the more embedded the behaviour becomes. It's important to stop the behaviour toward us, because it sends the person a very clear message about what we are willing to tolerate (we teach people how to treat us). Because we are all connected, refusing to accept that behaviour also helps all the other people in that person's life, both present and future. It solidifies our boundaries (for us and them), which helps in the "good fences make good neighbours" department and lays solid groundwork for the next person they attempt to control to stand on and stand up .

Most people actually feel better knowing exactly where their boundaries are with you because that clarifies their options and they don't have to guess. It also enables them to have a healthy respect for you that isn't fear based. Again, there can be no aggression and no attachment to the outcome. Depending on the situation, quietly walking away may be the best option. If you know that you have overstepped someone else's boundaries, examine why you opted for intimidation over affection or respect. Vulnerability is frightening but more rewarding. Conversely, if someone is trying to claim victim status just to make you look like a monster, calmly address the problem and/or refuse to participate. This is an example of liberalism in its truest sense.

"I won't let you walk all over me, but I won't condemn you for trying, because I don't know your story or what got you to this point."

"I won't blame you for laying down for me to walk all over, because I don't know your story or what got you to this point. Neither will I accept a role that makes me 'the bad guy' just to keep you comfortable and help maintain your victim status."

I would even go so far as to suggest that our inability to manifest liberalism in this way has precipitated most of the other political and social rifts present in our current society. When liberalism is done right, there's no need to look for other systems to compensate for shortcomings in the current social paradigm. The concept of tolerance is meant to allow other people to live their lives as they see fit; it is not meant to let people damage or destroy our lives. The tolerance you're asking for should not require me to behave in a way that is contrary to my values. We are all crucial parts of our environment, and that comes with great privileges and great responsibilities. Let's practice being good to each other, because we are all inextricably intertwined.

THE JOURNAL:

Think about someone who you have "wronged" or someone who has "wronged" you in the past. Try and re-evaluate the situation armed with the new insight you have from reading along and doing the exercises in the book thus far. Were you a victim? Were you a bully? How could you get through a similar situation by calmly and clearly stating your case without taking on the characteristics of either role? How can you stand up for yourself without making the other person feel small? How can you demonstrate respect while not losing your self-respect? How can you try to reveal your vulnerable side instead of trying to overpower people in your life? Take a few notes. Practice a few scenarios in your head and figure out a few non-negotiables, in case the scenario doesn't play out like it did in your rehearsal. Pick a couple of gems like "I will not raise my voice." "I will not hurl insults." "If I feel myself getting mad, I will breathe and count to ten."

These are general tools that you can use without knowing the precise details of how a conversation might unfold. Practice the *Ho'opono pono* if you have been wronged or done wrong. It can work both ways and helps to remind us to focus on connection, not separation.

LESSON 13:

NO MATTER WHAT OBSTACLES THERE ARE, THE FLOW OF THE CREEK (LIFE AND LEARNING) TO THE LAKE (GOALS SUCH AS HAPPINESS, SPIRITUAL GROWTH, INNER PEACE, ETC.) WILL ALWAYS RESUME.

I mentioned in Lesson 8 that, a couple of years ago, we had a pretty substantial drought in Southern Ontario. I said the creek looked much less like a creek and much more like a sporadic collection of mud puddles. The idea in this lesson is that even in those very dry conditions, the creek never stopped completely. Nor did it start going backwards up the side of the escarpment, and we don't do that either. We may get caught in a cycle (Lesson 7), but we don't go completely backwards. Whatever experiences you're having now, and whatever you've been through in the past conspire to prepare you for what you will face as your life goes on.

Even a circular-looking path will allow you to pick up different grains of sand each time you repeat the cycle. You may be able to bank different little tidbits of knowledge and experience that can help you the next time you're in a similar situation. Maybe your acquired knowledge will help someone else who's going through the same sort of thing. In ten years, you may need the experience you gained from being in three "bad" relationships with someone who's controlling. Not two relationships, but three. You may be accused of stubbornly repeating your patterns, but that repetition may prepare you to finally find the right relationship. You will possess not only the appreciation for someone who's good to you but also the attitude to stubbornly stay committed and make it work, in spite of potential baggage.

We are quick to look down our noses at people who we judge as obsessed or fanatical, but as soon they achieve some success, we praise them as being determined, dedicated and devoted. All of our personality traits can be viewed from a positive or negative perspective, and all our experiences contribute to the development of these characteristics. Maybe you needed to develop your stubborn streak over three bad relationships so you could develop the appreciation and conviction to stubbornly refuse to end the right relationship. It's all forward motion. We live, we learn, and we can't do one without the other. Some may appear to learn faster than others, but we all get there on our own schedule.

Looking at our experiences this way helps us to remove some of the sting from past hurts, because we start to recognize and appreciate the benefits of our lessons. This perspective also helps us to forgive ourselves and ease up on the frustration we may feel. I used to beat myself up on a regular basis for not being farther along. I always felt I should have better self-awareness by now, a better career by now, spiritual enlightenment by now, etc. You get the picture. Anything I could find to criticize myself about was fair game: too fast, too slow, too high, too low. As we have already discussed, you find what you look for, and I discovered a lot of material I could work with!

This is also a great example of criticism versus constructive criticism. Being hard on myself did absolutely nothing to help my situation, because there was no "constructive" part. To construct means "to build" and my negative self-talk was all about tearing myself down. Because so much criticism is offered these days from a place of insecurity or feeling threatened, we tend to attribute a negative attitude towards all criticism.

When constructive criticism is offered out of love, it will offer you those "Ah-ha!" moments. It will feel more like a helpful suggestion, and you will feel like "Yes! That's what my project needed!" or "Yes! That's what was missing from the soup!" It will aid your forward motion and can feel like a real relief, because something wasn't quite right and you couldn't put your finger on it. When someone says (as I was saying to myself), "That sucks!" or "You're so stupid!" or "You haven't learned anything!" there's a big difference! These types of sentiment do not aid your progress (and can often hinder it), because they're personal and vague and meant to be degrading. This is a prime example of when you can employ the strategies outlined in Lesson 12 and calmly say, "I would really appreciate any suggestions, if you have some good ideas about how I can improve or change what I'm working on. However, I won't tolerate your criticism unless it comes with some sound advice." Just remember, if you don't want to tolerate that behaviour from others, when talking to yourself, you're subject to the same rule!

Because I have always struggled to set healthy boundaries and keep my self-talk loving, I decided to employ my maternal instincts. I would think about some behaviour that I was questioning whether or not to accept (from someone else or myself), and try to decide if I would accept someone speaking to my daughters that way. We're usually a lot less tolerant for the people we're designed to protect, so it's a good gauge. I used to say to my ex, when he would mutter some disparaging remark about himself, "Hey! You're talking about the man I love!"

We're not socialized to protect and nurture ourselves. I don't mean pamper (although there's nothing wrong with a bit of that either!), I mean nurture. If you're getting a pedicure every other week but not spending time in quiet, daily reflection, you've got the pamper thing down but not the nurture, and the results will not be the same. Many therapists will tell you that, as a parent, you need to look after yourself first so you can be in a better place for your kids. This idea has some merit, but I still feel like it puts the focus on someone else. Parents tend to do that anyway. That's part of the problem!

Set your own goals. Start with small ones, so you can achieve them and revel in what that feels like. Accept where you are, but don't be satisfied. Don't beat yourself up for what you perceive as delays, but don't give up either. Delays are not necessarily denials. If you did the exercise in Lesson 1, you spent some time recognizing some things you like about yourself. Think about the ones you wrote down and uncover some more. If there are things you really don't like, ask the right questions. How can I stop doing this? What small step can I take in the direction of where I want to go? Choose to do one thing right now, and praise yourself when you've done it. Really feel proud of yourself and then ask, "What next?"

This is your journey and your creek. Contrary to how it may feel sometimes, you can't go backwards, and you shouldn't try. I recently saw a Facebook post that said something like, "Un-f*#k yourself. Be who you were before all the stuff happened that dimmed your shine." While I applaud the sentiment of regaining lost innocence and a trusting nature, I think it might be a little off the mark. If you spend your time trying to go back to being the person you were, you forsake the opportunity to be the person you can become. All of your experiences have combined to make you the person you are now. You don't have to go over your stories again and again. The benefit of those stories is already living in the person you've become. You will continue to grow and change with all the new experiences that are coming your way. So, take care of yourself. Accept, but don't settle. You may slow down, but you will keep going. Encourage yourself as you would a small child just learning how to walk, gently without judgement, and just watch you go!

THE JOURNAL:

Take some time, when you're feeling inspired (it's okay if that's not right now), to write a few things to your "feeling a bit down" self. There can be a huge temptation when everything is going well to neglect your due diligence in terms of spiritual nurturing. "Everything's good! I don't need to journal right now. I just use that for therapy!"

Well, due to the cyclical nature of our existence, I try to stockpile a few uplifting tidbits during the good times, so I have some fortifications on hand for the tougher times. I have a few feel-good movies (*The Blind Side* and *Invictus* are two goodies!), a special Spotify playlist, screenshots of some good Facebook memes, some inspirational quotes, and a couple of books that always bolster me a bit. Writing to yourself in a caring and compassionate manner with reassurance that things will get better and a description of how that will look and feel, is also a great tool to have in your arsenal.

So, this assignment is to write yourself a letter. If you struggle with the idea of being caring and compassionate to yourself, pretend you're writing to someone you care deeply about, or a beloved child who is pain, depressed or discouraged. What would you say to that dear friend? How would you console an upset child? How would you try and rally their spirits? What wonderful things would you say to reassure them? What would you tell them you love about them?

Write this letter at the back of your journal, so you always know where to find it. Even if the flow of the creek slows to a snail's pace, it will always resume, so let's get you back in the game!

LESSON 14:

THE FLOW OR PATH OF THE CREEK CAN SOMETIMES BE ALTERED BY OUTSIDE INFLUENCES, BUT IT CAN'T BE STOPPED ALTOGETHER.

Human beings became industrialized with the revolution between 1760–1840. That revolution seemed to bring with it an arrogance that humans could make things that were more efficient or "better" than Mother Nature. As a consequence, a certain amount of contempt developed for simpler methods. The "civilized" population regarded people as "savages" if they chose to forsake modern conveniences and work with Mother Nature as opposed to trying to tame her. We have mechanized, technologized, and chemicalized almost everything around us.

We're told by the innovators (who, coincidentally, are the ones who benefit financially) that all of this development is better for us. We will be safer, smarter and have more time. If you Google "cancer" or "stress," you can see how much information is available on just these two conditions. If you then investigate the increase in their occurrence over recent years, you might start to question the validity of this notion that all progress is beneficial. Strangely enough, one of the few elements on this planet that humans haven't "conquered" is water.

We can make it out into space, but we can't get to the very depths of the oceans. We can build skyscrapers almost 830 meters tall (that's 2,722 feet for my American friends) but preventing a leaky basement can still be a challenge. The eternal nature of water can be demonstrated by the number of bridges over, tunnels under, and vessels to float on its surface that we've built because we can't "conquer" water.

We can direct the flow to some extent, but we can't stop the flow altogether. Even the Hoover Dam has to let some water through or it will flood over. We can use the flow to our advantage, in producing hydroelectricity, but the flow remains unstoppable. This all ties into the last lesson, where we discussed that our progress is unstoppable, but this lesson is more about the human spirit and life itself being subject to relentless forward motion. If you try to stand still, life will move past you, and it will leave you behind.

The vast majority of us will, at some point, drop anchor to some event or person in our past. We will continue to move forward but will maintain the attachment to that person or event. When we have reached the end of our anchor rope, it will stretch and strain, giving us at best, a feeling of slowed progress or at worst, tremendous pain. Eventually, in either case, something will snap. It may be years later and leave us wondering what in our present life caused this inappropriate reaction to a minor event. The present event may be the trigger, but it's the anchor you dropped in the past and the relentless forward motion of life that has caused the stress.

Another, perhaps more positive, example of this natural law is the incarceration of Nelson Mandela. This man spent twenty-seven years in several South African prisons after being arrested for conspiring to overthrow the apartheid government in 1962. Much of his prison term was served in a tiny cell on Robben Island. I'm sure most of us would agree that this time would look like a complete stall in progress, and a twenty-seven year one at that!

Life, like the creek, did not come to a full stop for Nelson or South Africa. Mandela and his supporters managed to continue their struggle against apartheid in spite of his imprisonment. They won his freedom in 1990 and subsequently his presidency in 1994. Life must have moved very slowly for Nelson Mandela over the course of those twenty-seven years but move it did. He was able to use that time to figure out how to forgive his captors but also to figure out how to start to resolve the racial dissonance in the country he loved. Life moved on, and Nelson Mandela refused to let a twenty-seven-year incarceration keep him from moving forward with it.

Progress is yet another situation where people may mistake what they have a choice about. Life, like the creek, is unstoppable. The only choice you have regarding the forward movement of your life is how you are going to approach that forward movement, not whether or not you are subject to it. Life goes on, the saying tells us, and it does so whether you're riding the current or kicking and screaming. You get to choose your rate of progress but not the option of progress.

THE JOURNAL:

What ties do you have to your past? This is a big question, so take a bit of time to answer. What still makes your stomach turn when you think about it? What did you do, or what did someone else do, that you haven't forgiven? If you say you've forgiven (yourself or someone else), but there's still pain associated with the person or event, you're kidding yourself. True forgiveness will release you from your pain, and the memory that's left, once the associated emotions are gone, will become part of your wisdom library.

I won't lie to you. This will be a tough, but you created a solid base in Lesson 9, so let's put that to work. Look into the dark parts and shed some light on things you've buried to try and stop the pain. Forgive the person involved—yourself included. Do the *Ho'opono pono*. Write a letter to the person and burn it. Let it go. Say this out loud, as you're lighting your letter on fire: "I release you, my pain, my guilt, my attachment to you, my attachment to this event, my anger, my self-pity, my self-righteousness..."

Dig deep!! Drag all that stuff up to the surface, light it up, and let it go. Although these constricting emotions lie in the shadows, they are closer to the surface than most people think. You can't bury them, you need to wade through them with a floodlight. This is the only way to get deep down to the positive emotions like joy, peace, love and gratitude. Consider that most of us can go from zero to irate in the split-second it takes for someone to cut us off in traffic, but we can spend eternity trying to rekindle a feeling of love for someone who wronged us. The "negative" emotions actually lie closer to the surface, so when we try to bury them, we actually bury the "positive" emotions even further down. Only the stuff that you try to avoid or ignore has any power over you. You need to dissipate those constricting surface emotions through acknowledgement, to be able to feel the deeper, positive ones. Shine your light, accept what you see, feel it to deal with it and then send your release up in flames, so you can continue with your relentless forward motion, unencumbered.

LESSON 15:

EVEN THOUGH WE WATER DROPLETS ARE ALL FLOWING IN THE SAME CREEK WITH THE SAME PERCEIVED DIRECTION, EACH OF US DIFFER IN MANY WAYS.

WE ALL HAVE A DIFFERENT COLLECTION OF EXPERIENCES THAT MAKE US UNIQUE.

WE'RE ALL TOGETHER IN THIS CREEK AND FOLLOW THE SAME GENERAL RULES OF NATURE, BUT WE'RE NOT ALL THE SAME. EQUAL, BUT NOT THE SAME.

This lesson excites me! I just love the fact that we all have so many similarities and so many differences at the same time. I started travelling by myself when I was relatively young, and the similarities between the culture I left and the first one I visited certainly offered some comfort and security to a naive young traveller. The differences though... The differences were where it really got interesting! Some differences were language based and made communication quite comical at times. Some differences were dietary in nature, and for anyone who has travelled to exotic destinations and tried local cuisine, you know that just having dinner can be an adventure in itself. Some differences were cultural, habit, or rule based, like driving on the left-hand side of the road. All of these differences made it quite interesting to explore new ideas.

As I said in Lesson 11, the main thing that makes us unique is the particular collection of ideas and experiences that we gather over the course of our lives. Which ideas you hear and decide to incorporate, or which ones become less important, make each of us who we are. I jokingly say that I am never too proud to steal a good idea if someone is willing to share one!

My experience is unique, because I may use a concept that I learned in agricultural college to help me learn how to fly helicopters. First of all, there may not be another person alive who went to the same college as I did, the same year as I did, and went to the same flight school as I did. Even if there were another person who did those things, they may not have had the same teachers, same curriculum, same majors, same schedule, etc. So, what information I was offered, when it was offered, how it was presented and by whom, are all variables that influenced what pieces I decided to take away. Then you can also factor in whether there was a cute boy sitting beside me in class, or a talkative friend, whether I had been out drinking the night before, or maybe I just wasn't feeling well, and you get an idea of just how many variables are involved in making us unique.

Our individuality is one of the things that makes us each amazing, and we need to share our awesome so that others aren't afraid to share theirs. If we are brave enough to be vulnerable with our own authenticity, and remove the temptation to be critical of theirs, people around us feel more comfortable being themselves, and we get the benefit of being witness to their particular brand of wonder. Marianne Williamson puts it beautifully in her book *A Return to Love: Reflections on the Principles of "A Course in Miracles."*

> *"Our deepest fear is not that we are inadequate. Our deepest fear is that we are powerful beyond measure. It is our light, not our darkness that most frightens us. We ask ourselves, 'Who am I to be brilliant, gorgeous, talented, fabulous?' Actually, who are you not to be? You are*

a child of God. Your playing small does not serve the world. There is nothing enlightened about shrinking so that other people won't feel insecure around you. We are all meant to shine, as children do. We were born to make manifest the glory of God that is within us. It's not just in some of us; it's in everyone. And as we let our own light shine, we unconsciously give other people permission to do the same. As we are liberated from our own fear, our presence automatically liberates others."

This sentiment can be demonstrated repeatedly throughout history, but since I'm a runner, I will use an example from running. Many people know that Roger Bannister was the first man to break the four-minute mile in May of 1954. This was an important accomplishment, because until then, it was commonly believed that it was physically impossible for humans to break that barrier. What many people don't know is that by the end of May, 1955, four other men had also broken the four-minute mile. Roger and a man named John Landy both actually ran a sub-four twice that same year!

Some people suggest that these statistics prove that the psychological barrier is just as important, if not more so, than any perceived physical limitations, while others don't agree. What I find exciting is how fantastic accomplishments can spark our imaginations and expand our beliefs about what's possible. As Marianne says, once we get out from under our own fear, it can help others around us to get out from under theirs!

This works because of the similarities we share with our fellow water droplets. Look for things that resonate with you, but don't think that everything about a person, a belief system or a career has to. It's great to meet someone who has an idea that rings true for us. They share and we think, *Yes! Yes! That's how I feel!* We can certainly learn from each other, build some enthusiasm and firm up our foundation when we share similar ideas.

If that same person then says something that sounds like "two plus two equals five" to you, it's okay to not agree with that part, even if you liked the first thing they said. Loving someone doesn't mean agreeing with everything they say. Disagreeing with someone doesn't mean you have to hate them. The same view and a different view can both be celebrated, and agreeing to differ is sometimes the only thing that makes peace possible.

To really achieve peace, I feel we need to address the concept of equality. It seems so simple, but our society really struggles with this concept and its implementation. Of course, the idea will likely be pooh-poohed by those among us who rely on putting other people down to gain power or make themselves feel better. Quite often though, I feel the idea of true equality is also dismissed by those who purport to be fighting for it. I hear many groups fighting for equality, but when you examine their platforms a little closer, what they're really after is to be treated as if they're special. There seems to be much more emphasis on our differences than on our similarities.

I think this situation has developed because our working definition of equality is failing. When someone talks about equality these days, there's often a general tone of "you're no better than I am" infused in their argument. It encourages an atmosphere of repression and oppression. Why would any person or group pursue that? It's not like stifling your development will set me free. When going through a challenge, we must also resist the temptation to insist that our situation is so different that, when people try to help, we alienate them. If I respond to your offer by suggesting that I am going through something you couldn't possibly understand, you feel snubbed, belittled, unappreciated and misunderstood. The differences in my situation are not a valid excuse to remain a victim. We can learn so much if we look for similarities and use the tools that a friend may be offering. Some strategies work for humans. Period. Just because a program or support group works for a large number of people, doesn't mean you're not special when it works for you too. I propose that we adopt a little shift in our attitude and think more like "I'm amazing and so are you!"

The difference that other people will feel when you come from this place is important, but it also allows you to expand and accept your own awesomeness. It's a true win-win! I also feel that this will encourage everyone to strive for real equality, because who wouldn't want to be amazing? Often times those who demand acceptance refuse to offer it. Someone else's acceptance of you cannot replace your acceptance of yourself. If you don't have acceptance for yourself, you don't have it to give anyone else either. Appreciating your own awesome nature is essential; just don't let it end there.

Once people can feel truly valued for who they are without conditions or competition, they are liberated to offer love instead of shoring up their defences. Once people feel appreciated and respected for what they're good at, they may be a little more willing to concede what they're not good at. Once we realize that we can love someone and not like everything they say, that we can have enormous respect for someone even if they're not good at everything, and that we can accept (ourselves and others) without necessarily approving, equality can take hold and grow.

The peace that comes with equality can require some work from everyone concerned, and I feel like there are a few dynamics that can be addressed to help resolve some of the most common issues:

1. I have an iPhone. I really don't know too much about phones, but it seemed like a logical choice for me when I got it. There are a *lot* of people who have iPhones, and phone choice can spark a lot of controversy. I-people can have the tendency to look down their noses at non-I-people. It's almost like "Anyone who's anyone has an iPhone. What's wrong with you?"

I suspect there's some proprietary tech that promotes that rift a little. "Oh, you can't get my pics on your phone? Maybe you should get a phone like mine." Apple has created a technological culture like no one else. So, all of a sudden, it becomes a bit of an "us and them" situation. Over *phones!* The other thing that happens is that Galaxy-man, being defensive about coming under fire for not being an I-person, starts to take on a sort of smug, superior air. "Oh, you're one of the I-flock? Too bad you don't actually know anything about technology, or you'd realize how much better it is to be a Galaxy-man. You're clearly just a lemming who can't resist peer pressure or a well-targeted ad campaign. I'm too smart to fall for that garbage."

Then there's just a lot of "Na-na-na-na-na! My phone's better than your phone!" It's like the owners built the things themselves or something. Advertising is the main culprit in promoting this type of attitude. "You can be the envy of all your friends!" I don't want my friends to envy me. I want them to love and support me! And I want to do the same for them. I don't want them to want what I have. I want them to want what *they* have. Similarities: We both have phones that we love. Differences: I have an iPhone; you have a Samsung Galaxy. I'm happy with my phone. I hope you're happy with your phone. And if I have pics that I can't text, I'll email them. Done.

2. I'm vegan. Vegans can be pretty judgey. I don't mean the "I can't eat meat because I hate the thought of killing animals." I mean the "You eat animals?? You're a murderer!!" If you happen to be a non-vegan, I don't think you get to be offended by the first statement, but you certainly get to take issue with the second! If I spend time with meat-eaters who ask (and before I say anything that might be considered pontificating, they *have* to *ask),* I will tell them why I don't eat meat. If they don't ask, I'll ask them what kind of music they like, if they run, or if they have a motorcycle. I practice a vegan diet. It's how I choose to eat. It's not everything I am. If we take the time to look or ask, we can find things in common, so why focus on the differences unless we're going to learn from them or celebrate them?

3. I'm an author and a helicopter pilot. I have no idea how to run the electrical in my new house. I wouldn't want to mess around with that either, so I need someone who knows electrical. Maybe I can find an electrician who wants to take his family sightseeing in a helicopter. He needs a pilot! We are equal but not the same. It's what the barter system was founded and then built on. We have skills that may be equally desirable or necessary, but they're different skills. Thank goodness! We wouldn't get too far as a society if we were all pilots! If we are both doing what we are good at, we're both following our soul's purpose and contributing to the betterment of humanity. Appreciation and respect for our differences helps everyone get what they need, while acknowledging that we are all the same in our desire to be heard and seen.

So, we can all be going in the same direction, but through our interactions with other droplets and our surroundings, we become unique and beautiful members of the same creek, each of us just as important as any other.

THE JOURNAL:

Is there something you do that not many people know you do? Is there something about any of your friends that is really different and cool? Do you love ballroom dancing? Does a friend play the oboe? Write down a couple things that make you unique, and then a couple things that make some of your friends unique. Think about how cool these different hobbies, talents and skills are. I may be an avid lawn bowler, and you may be an avid skateboarder. Our hobbies and skills make us different. If we both love what we do, that makes us the same.

Let's celebrate how cool and how important we both are for different reasons. Ask your friends what they love about what they do. This will inform you and remind them. Write down what you think our world might be like without your type of talent. Happiness comes from doing what we're good at, and satisfaction comes from knowing our contributions are significant. There may be many people doing what you do, and we need every one of you. No one does it like you, and you don't do it like the person next to you. Different but equal.

LESSON 16:

THE CREEK WE LIVE IN IS NOT THE ONLY CREEK.

IT MAY BE THE ONE WHERE WE FEEL MOST COMFORTABLE, BUT THERE ARE MANY MORE CREEKS.

MAYBE WE'LL ALL MEET WHEN WE MAKE IT TO OUR DESTINATION, NO MATTER IF WE CALL THAT THE LAKE, SEA, ENLIGHTENMENT, HEAVEN OR WHATEVER.

Oh boy! This is a big one! And applicable to so many issues going on in the world today. As a water droplet, our creek—actually the little part of the creek where we're at—seems like all there is. As we move along, we figure out that there is so much more! More to our creek, more creeks, more water droplets, and many more possibilities than just those within arm's reach. We realize that time (the creek bed) contains us to a certain extent, but it changes as we go along. Think about what an eternity five minutes feels like when you're five, and how it flies when you're fifty-five.

We realize that there's an ebb and flow to all of life's processes. We realize that some water droplets may travel with us for just a short time, and some may travel with us for most of our journey. We realize that some water droplets have travelled different paths, picked up different grains of sand, touched the bottom of the creek bed at different points, or travelled at the top of the water flow. In the big picture, we are all in this creek together, and this is our creek.

Now, with the help of technology, most of us also realize that there are many other creeks out there. Some are bigger, some smaller, but the experience of being water droplets in a creek has certain universal similarities.

For all the past and present physics students out there, we know by experience and experiment that water will always behave in one of just a few ways. If you change one little variable, water may behave a little differently, but it always follows certain patterns, and there are always things that water won't do. What we focus on is where our energy goes, and consequently, what decides our future. I (and my fellow creek-dwelling water droplets) may do things in the creek where my journey takes place that you don't do in the creek where your journey takes place. Due to minor variables, you may do things in your creek that I don't, and that's ok.

The minute my focus turns to what you do that I don't, and I decide that makes you and your fellow droplets wrong, inferior or "bad," then we have a problem. What about all the things we do the same? We all flow downstream, we all progress toward our goal, we all hit some rocks occasionally, and we all pick up a grain of sand or two. If we criticize the droplets in the creek next door for doing one thing differently, don't we run the risk of being criticized for one different little thing also? Condemned possibly, for one little thing?

Would you do the same thing in that creek? Can you possibly know that? If the water droplets in the creek next door go over a cliff as a waterfall, are you going to sit in your comfortable sea-level creek, pointing your watery finger, thinking, *Oooh! Look at those droplets acting all fast and loose ... flying through the air!* Wouldn't you have to do the same thing in that situation? Again, it's about acceptance and respect, especially when considering the actions of people who are in a situation you know nothing about.

I think back to when Hurricane Katrina rocked New Orleans in 2005. The subsequent devastation and flooding were far-reaching, but some of the hardest hit wards were also the poorest. There was a lot of controversy over whether help was slow in coming due to this fact. Then the news coverage started, and there were many video clips of people fighting over bottled water, raiding shops for food, and desperately trying to get their families to safety. Many residents had to be rescued because they "refused" to leave their homes.

There was a general attitude of looking-down-noses directed toward the people who ended up at the Louisiana Superdome, because "they were acting like animals." Residents who had to be rescued, were criticized for staying when they knew Katrina was coming. Critical judgement was running rampant from many people who didn't really know what was going on. When the truth of what was happening finally started to come out, it was horrifying. Residents were not warned in time, as many were without a vehicle, poor and looking after dependants. Many didn't have anywhere to go, felt that they had weathered many storms before, and were led to believe this forecasted Category 3 hurricane (when it made landfall) wouldn't be any different. There wasn't sufficient food, water or sanitation to supply the almost 20,000 people that eventually made their way to the Superdome, and when the 170 mph winds started peeling the roof off like the top of a tuna can, things went from bad to worse. Throw in flooding at field level and 90-degree temperatures, and anyone can see that this was a recipe for disaster.

My point in sharing all of this is that so many were very quick to criticize, like they would never stoop to that level. Really? Your six-month-old baby hasn't had water (or formula, or breast milk because you too, are so dehydrated) in a day or so, and you wouldn't fight to get them some? You wouldn't fight to keep your disabled mother from dying in front of you? There was almost an attitude of disgust from some people, who felt something like this could never happen to them, because these people chose this by living in that location.

When we focus more on the similarities we have, we can empathize with people who might have one or two small differences. We realize that, as humans, we are going to respond to any given situation in one of a couple different ways, and trust that, in the same situation, we would likely do the same things to survive. From there, we can get to the place of trying to feel how desperate we would have to be to resort to that behaviour, and realize that those people (our fellow water droplets) must be feeling that desperate also.

This part hurts, I know, and we have to do it anyway. Judgement and subsequent criticism are often employed by us to distance ourselves from something awful. We don't want to think about what it would feel like to be in that situation, so we use judgement and criticism to delude ourselves into thinking we have control. If we can convince ourselves we have control over our lives, we can also tell ourselves that we would never "allow" ourselves to be put in that situation. Most of us don't actually have any idea how to create our outer reality, so we really can't exercise control over outside events or the variables that create different situations. We need to practice understanding over contempt.

Every. Single. Time.

You can even tell yourself that you don't think you would make the same choices in the same situation (of course, you can't truly know until you're there), but if the focus is on our similarities instead, we can have compassion for the people actually in the situation. Compassion doesn't mean tolerating behaviour that might hurt other us or other people, it means understanding that a fellow water droplet must have been feeling horrible pain and desperation to act that way. When you start thinking about what you think you'd do or wouldn't do, you have taken the focus from them and put it back on you.

Another impediment to focusing on our similarities is our need to feel special, and our tendency to look outside ourselves to have that need met. We talked about equality in Lesson 15, and this a different facet of the same issue. You are special, not "better than", special. We are ALL special, and no one knows how true that is for you, better than you.

So, stop looking for other people to give you the confirmation that you're not giving yourself. If you don't think you're worth your time, why would they? If you're waiting for an enlightened soul to recognize your value, it won't serve as a substitute for self-worth, and it puts the focus on our differences. There is strength in numbers, and if we can all get together based on our similarities, we are unstoppable. We can have compassion and faith based on our similarities without losing our individuality. You don't have to act different. You *are* different.

We are each a unique expression of the Universe/God/Higher Power, and we are all connected by our experience of that unique expression taking place in human form. Our individuality and our connectedness are both qualities of equal value. Neither one should be sacrificed to try and gain more of the other. It is not only our differences that make us who we are, it is our similarities also. Let's celebrate both!

THE JOURNAL:

Think about how you identify yourself. It is one theme in Buddhist meditation to ask yourself (repeatedly), "Who am I?" So, ask yourself this question. I am a middle-class, middle-aged, Canadian woman. In truth, this statement is more about what I make, how many years I've had on this planet, where I was born, and what gender I identify with, than who I actually am, but for the moment, we'll just say this is who I am.

Think about someone/some group who is vastly different from you. The differences should be obvious, be they cultural, gender, species or belief based. Write down the person/group that you have picked, and then write down five or so similarities. How are you like a Muslim male? How are you like a dolphin? How are you like an Asian child? How are you like a water droplet in a creek? Differences can be pretty easy to spot, so look for similarities. When you identify these, compassion, understanding and love come much more easily.

LESSON 17:

THE POOLS THAT FORM IN THE CREEK BED WHEN THERE HASN'T BEEN A LOT OF RAIN CAN BE LOOKED UPON AS TIMES TO PREPARE RATHER THAN JUST TO REST AND BECOME COMPLACENT.

THESE POOLS OFTEN FORM BEFORE A ROCKY BIT OF THE CREEK'S JOURNEY, SO GATHERING YOUR STRENGTH AND MENDING ANYTHING THAT MIGHT BE BROKEN IS A BETTER IDEA THAN JUST RESTING ON YOUR LAURELS.

The first part of this book came pretty easily for me. In fact, I didn't feel like it had been *me* writing it at all, more like the Universal Consciousness expressing itself *through* me. Then life got busy with everyday tasks, and I hit a bit of a wall. Nothing was *wrong*; I just wasn't being very proactive about my existence and purpose. Things were reasonably comfortable, and so I settled into the pattern of day to day. I was resting on my laurels and the Universe responded (after several gentler nudges) by yanking the rug out from under me.

My husband of twenty years left me for a younger woman. She was a client of his and a "friend" of mine. I was heartbroken and shattered. How did this happen to two people who had committed to be together forever? Situations like this are all too common in our society's present climate, and the frequency with which they occur tends to diminish (if not entirely negate) compassion for the people left behind. The damage to my family, the loss of friends, the destruction of my self-confidence, and the loneliness that ensued almost destroyed me.

I have always said that when one person in a relationship has an affair, both parties in that relationship share responsibility. Now I was left with the weight of that belief. It was weeks before I could even begin to consider what lessons were hidden in this experience. His role and his actions were abundantly obvious, but what part did I need to take responsibility for? After many tears, conversations with a few good friends and family (my younger daughter was a rock!), and some serious soul searching, I started to figure it out.

My ex-husband and I were in a pool before a rocky patch, and neither of us used that time to build each other up or invest in our relationship. We both got lazy, watching endless reruns on TV, letting some distance develop between us, letting our communication lapse, and forgetting how much we valued each other. All I could do was assess my part, as his choices and actions were his to reconcile.

Don't get me wrong, I had been busy. My daughter and I were less than a year in to a new restaurant, I was a few hours away from getting my pilot's licence, and we were trying to plan for our future, but we were together, and I took that for granted. A relationship is a living, changing, hopefully growing thing, and I was starving mine. That pool we were in was a perfect opportunity to feed and invest in us. I was busy but there was no trauma, there were no fires to put out, and no major life events that required our attention to the exclusion of everything else.

It would have been a perfect time to reinvent date night, find a new activity that we could do together, or just show each other that we both still cared. Instead, we both focused on what we weren't getting, and as a result, a beautiful partnership slipped right through our fingers. If this sounds like regret, it's not. I was also guilty of not setting healthy boundaries and enabling toxic relationships. Had I been able to use my time in the pool for reflection and self-development, things probably would have turned out much differently. We most likely would have still split up, but I would have been much better prepared and much less devastated. I know that everything needed to happen the way it did, and I am grateful to my ex and his new wife for freeing me from a small life. My "flood" from the Universe was necessary, because I was complacent in my pool.

You'll know when you hit a pool like this, because you will feel it. You will feel comfortable, or you'll feel a little uneasy, like you're waiting for the other shoe to drop. You may find yourself trying to justify that everything's okay because there's nothing really *wrong*. If you have been in survival mode for a long time, it feels a little strange, because there's no immediate threat. This can be the perfect time to switch to thrive mode. You can adopt habits now, like meditation, tail chi or journaling, which will carry you through future rough patches. Putting these habits into place now, while you have time, will make them easier to maintain when things get crazy. Then, when you really need the benefits of these practices, you'll not only have the growth you've accomplished in the pool, you'll have a schedule that already includes time for these things.

If you hit such a pool in your journey along the creek, by all means pause to rest, regroup, and catch your breath, but don't think for a minute that you'll get to stay there. We droplets in the creek are subject to relentless forward motion, however slow. Life is cyclical in nature, so take stock and repair. Take those very important breaks in what can seem like chaos. Build-up, strengthen, and reinvest in yourself, the people around you, and your relationships with them. The rocky bits that may be around the corner are easily navigated, if you're solid in yourself and your people.

THE JOURNAL:

Refer back to your notes from Lesson 7 and recall what you said you'd like to do if money were no object. If there are things on that list that you haven't taken the first steps toward, revisit how you might proceed when you're in a pool. Doing things you love or think you'll love is great self-care for your inner, fun-loving child. Then make a new list of practices you can adopt during rest and recoup times that will help you over the rocky bits. Things like meditation, tail chi, walks in nature, date-nights, coffee dates with friends... All of these things can help immensely when life gets chaotic.

 Pick one to start with, and when that has become a solid part of your schedule, pick something else to add to the first practice. Remember that what you did to survive the last tough time won't help you to thrive when times are good. When you're no longer in a position where it's all you can do to tread water, taking a swimming lesson to improve your stroke may be helpful for the next time you're in a tough spot.

LESSON 18:

THINGS THAT ARE GOOD FOR THE CREEK AS A WHOLE ARE USUALLY BENEFICIAL TO THE WATER DROPLETS IN THE CREEK AS WELL.

The good of the many outweighs the good of the few. It's usually a sentiment heard in some sci-fi or apocalypse-type movie when some poor individual has to die to save the rest of mankind. This isn't really what I'm talking about here. I'm talking about things being good for the creek's health probably being good for the individual water droplets as well. Picture it as something like "spreading the wealth."

This may seem a little socialist in nature, but having too much can be just as damaging as not having enough. Working too hard is as damaging as not working enough. If you're doing something (or not doing something) that you have to justify, then it's probably not the right thing. If you start any explanation off with the words "I deserve… because I…" then there's a good chance you have some issues around whatever that is. It means you're trying to figure out why you should have something that other people don't have, or how to make it ok to have something that normally isn't ok to have.

I find it helpful to consider what I might want that, if I got it, everyone else would get it too. Perhaps I would like a new sports car, so now everyone else in Grimsby gets one too. Well, I love driving fast, well-built cars, so whether or not everyone else also has one doesn't matter to me. If I was hoping to have the car to get attention, then I probably wouldn't want everyone else to have one, because then no one would notice mine. I may think that having more or having better is going to make me feel good because I have something my friends don't, but if my friends are struggling, it really doesn't. Even if we work really hard, even if we do some fast talking to our sub-conscious, we are all spiritually connected, not competitive.

Now, I know that some of you will feel like you're not going to work your asses off to buy some lounge-about a new sports car, but I don't mean giving your hard-earned dollars to a bunch of free-loaders. The other critical part of the equation is that no one slacks, and we all always do our best. People who seem to put a lot of thought into how they can do the least they can do aren't happy either. Some people think they don't want to work hard, but we were built to do just that. The trick is to find your passion and do that with unbridled enthusiasm and reckless abandon.

So, now you may be saying that it's probably no one's passion, for example, to collect garbage. That may be true, but imagine how different garbage collectors would feel about their jobs if they were given respect for their invaluable contribution to our society. Most of us need our garbage collectors much more often than we need our doctors or lawyers, so maybe we need to rethink our social hierarchy or do away with it all together. The people at the top of the hierarchy tend to fight the idea of this equalization the most, because they feel like they will lose their superiority. What they don't realize is what they will gain. What's good for the people is truly good for *all* the people. Sometimes, we just don't know what's good for us, so we keep pursuing more of what wasn't working, thinking that eventually, something will miraculously change. In a society where real mutual respect and equality are practiced by everyone, all members are valued and appreciated. The few at the top may lose their perceived superiority (which they never really had, anyway), but they also lose the need to keep up appearances because everyone gains an individually based sense of value and worth.

A few groups get this concept, and they keep to themselves by starting communes or similar closed social groups. The people who live atop the social hierarchy call them hippies or cults. There are certainly cults operating in our society, but you can tell them apart because they still operate from a hierarchy, and the leaders are tyrannical, or at least dictatorial in nature. Cults argue that their hierarchy is better than the rest of the world's, but it's still just another hierarchy.

I'm talking about groups of like-minded individuals with a variety of skill-sets getting together to give and take equally. Everybody works, everybody shares in the fruits of the group's labours, and based on a barter-style system, everybody is equal, just not the same.

My ex-husband and I used to trade shoes from our store for wine from a friend who is a vineyard owner. Right? What a great deal!! Once money was removed from the equation, things went quite smoothly. The Bible says that money is the root of all evil, and I tend to agree. Money is problematic, because it is non-perishable. This encourages people to save it. They save more than they need for longer than they need it.

If you had turnips, you couldn't keep them for years or they would go rotten. This means you are more likely to grow what you need, and if you have the good fortune of having a bumper crop, you might even share with your neighbours. In turn, they are more likely to share their good fortune with you. You might even discuss your planned crop with your neighbours, so you all have something different to share. This is all stuff that the upper hierarchy does not want happening. Money is a business, just like war, just like oil, just like healthcare, and the government has its hand in all of them. The barter system ensures that everyone involved in a transaction feels needed and respected. "I have something you need, and you have something I need. Let's talk."

Money encourages those who have it to take advantage of those who don't and then feel powerful because of that disparity. "I have fifty dollars, and you have none, so I'll give you a dollar, because it means very little to me, and you'll do almost anything for it, because it means a lot to you." Due to the non-perishable nature of that dollar, I can threaten you if you try to maintain your self-respect. If you refuse to do something unreasonable, I can threaten to keep the dollar. Then I wait for some other poor soul, who's just a bit hungrier or more desperate, and get him to do it. In this way, a sense of desperation or lack of self-respect is rewarded with the dollar, and of course that is a slippery slope. The "haves" reward the "have-nots" for having less and less in terms of finances, resources and self-respect, and this is how we find ourselves in our present social crisis.

The other advantage of the barter system is that it eliminates the tendency money has to create distance. People who have a lot of money often succumb to the temptation of throwing it around. Throwing money at a charity by writing a cheque or donating online is easy. It's much easier to throw money at someone and tell them to fix themselves. It's much easier than getting to know someone and their plight. It's much easier than getting in the trenches and figuring out what people really need. It's much easier than hearing people's stories and realizing that some little twist of fate could have landed you in the very same position. It's much easier to throw self-respect sucking, soul-destroying money at them while you try to absolve your guilt by telling yourself that you're helping.

What many people don't realize is that, because we are all connected, if you are feasting while others are starving, you won't feel good about that. Then you think you need more, but what you actually need is less, and to create less in your life by sharing with others. Creating more distance won't help.

This distance that money creates also leaves room for the middleman. The middleman operates in that shadowy terrain that exists between the haves and the have-nots, and for this, he exacts a fee. The middleman separates and distances people and then gets paid by the people he distances and separates. This is not just manufacturers trying to sell more, it also includes the big business of organized charities. Isn't this an oxymoron?

There are people making six figures who take money from people making less than half that, to give it to people making a tiny fraction of that and calling it charity. This happens because of the distance created by the existence of money. Even the good intentioned, well-meaning, compassionate people with money don't know how to help, because they've lost touch with the people that might need it. This happens when compassion dies at the hands of separation and distance.

If we want to remove the power money has in our present social paradigm, we must demand equal pay for equal effort. When we punish someone with lower wages because they were unable to afford a post-secondary education, it sets a vicious cycle into motion. That person's children may not be able to afford a post-secondary education either, not because of their aptitude or intellect but because of the income level of the family they were born into. In order to affect a change, we must award equal pay for equal effort instead of equal occupation, not just across the gender binary, not just across racial diversity, not just across municipal boundaries, but across the whole world.

This is a big step, and it will require many little steps. It will also mean that we, who have the privilege of living in an incredibly affluent country, may not be able to travel to sunny and warm, less-affluent countries just to take advantage of them. We may not be able to outsource our production of goods because foreign labour is cheaper. If we like travelling to the warm weather every winter, or building foreign production plants, we might have to start paying them what we think *we're* worth. Or maybe we'll just have to stay home and tend the turnip patch.

Because we're all connected, most people really want to help and feel guilty if we're not. Guilt is the Universe's call to action, and when you're not sure how to answer, organized charities are more than happy to take advantage of your feelings of helplessness. They will take your money, tell you what a great thing you've done, and give only a fraction to the people who really need it. The middleman jacks up the prices of everything you want or need, so he makes a lot of money and you feel like you're paying the manufactures, farmers, and service providers what their goods and services are worth.

On the other end, many people who refuse to work feel like they're not hurting anyone, because they just get a cheque in the mail, or an automatic deposit in their bank account every month. It's really all just smoke and mirrors. Imagine what would happen if someone in need got help from a person who could look them in the eye and offer one-on-one compassion. Imagine what would happen if a farmer got paid (or something traded) from someone who could look her in the eye with appreciation for what she does. Imagine what would happen if someone who refused to work had to look whoever they were getting help from in the eye, and appreciate that the person helping worked hard to be able to offer the help. Having money is not a crime. Using the possession of money to create a feeling of superiority and foster contempt for those who have not shared your good fortune, contributes to the separation that is eroding our society.

The distance between us creates anonymity and isolation. People try to stop caring about what's happening to their fellow water droplets, because it can become too painful when you care. The emotional, physical, and spiritual health of our world is in catastrophic decline. This needs to change, because what's good for the creek is good for all the droplets in the creek.

THE JOURNAL:

This isn't really a journal exercise, although you can write down some ideas, so you don't forget. Think of strategies you can employ to close the gap between the haves and the have-nots. Could you volunteer at a soup kitchen? Could you buy a couple sandwiches when you get your lunch and give them to a couple homeless people? Could you buy from the people who actually make or grow the things you need? Could you try and make a loaf of bread to see what it's actually worth to you? Could you make muffins for your garbage collector/letter carrier/roofer, etc.? What can you do to close the gap and start caring and connecting?

LESSON 19:

WATER DROPLETS, WHEN JOINED TOGETHER, CAN SUSTAIN LIFE OR DESTROY IT.

WE HAVE THE CHOICE WHICH OPTION WE WILL PICK.

Together we are very powerful. This can be called teamwork or herd mentality with different implications associated with each term. The choice of which position we align with is ours. We will get into a bit of "what energy you put out is what you attract," but more than that, we have to accept, acknowledge, and embrace not only our power but also the responsibility that goes with it.

As I write about this lesson, we have had record setting spring rainfall. I decided to head down to the creek to see what was happening. What I saw, while not unexpected, was awe-inspiring. The creek was full and fast and raging. A sight like that always leaves me in a state of wonder at the raw power possessed by Mother Nature, and as the creek had been so generous with its wisdom of late, I decided to pause awhile and see if it might pass along another gem.

I realized, as I watched, that the power and rage were quite exhilarating, exciting, and addictive. Even casually observing the process sent my heart-rate racing, caused my breath to catch in my throat, and glued me to my spot on the bank. And I was just watching. We are all susceptible to the frenzied contagion of an emotional outpouring by a group of our peers. This can translate two ways: in a brainstorming, "expanding on an idea" sort of way; or in a riotous, downward spiralling, "trampling fans at a soccer game," sort of way.

In Lesson 15, we talked about how Roger Bannister's achievements broke barriers and gave others permission to do the same. Sir Isaac Newton also alluded to this connection when he referred to the twelfth-century philosopher, Bernard of Chartres' sentiment, by saying, "If I have seen further, it is by standing on the shoulders of giants." It is thought that the giants Newton was referring to in his letter to Robert Hooke were Copernicus, Kepler and Galileo, amazing scientists whose discoveries spanned decades and provided a solid foundation upon which Newton was able to base his own history-making insights. This illustrates the idea that teamwork can even stretch across centuries, combining each person's talents to make the "team" stronger than any of its members would have been on their own.

The first "seed" (see Lesson 11) enables the next step in the evolution of an idea, and the person who comes up with the next idea humbly acknowledges and appreciates the contribution of the first seed. In this approach, we can have and create incredible power. Feed others and trust that you will also be fed. Support others and trust that you will also be supported. Humility, appreciation, and respect provide the foundation for the responsibility that inevitably comes with such power.

In herd mentality, there is certainly power associated with making each other stronger, but usually when someone moves up the ladder, the bottom rung gets knocked off in a Darwinian fashion, reflecting a "survival of the fittest" mentality. Due to the fear of being knocked off, the lower rungs will often create opposition to fellow members achieving great things. In this way, the whole herd, while having strength in numbers, is limited by its own members as to what it can accomplish.

Eventually, a predominant atmosphere of tearing down rather than building up develops. Members are afraid to build each other up because no one wants to be the bottom rung. There may be respect (out of fear) for other members, but the appreciation and humility are lacking, so there is a corresponding lack of responsibility. Using the post-game-riot analogy, there are certainly some fans who get pretty excited just watching the game at home by themselves, but would they trample another individual or loot a local shop by themselves? Probably not. That happens when energy is escalated in a group setting, and one's voice of reason gets drowned out by the roar of the crowd.

If we choose the "building each other up" avenue for our potential and power, there is also an honesty piece required that is based in respect. Support isn't telling someone that they can do something just because they want to and you're afraid to disappoint or anger them. I may have unrealistic dreams of being an Olympic gymnast, and you may think you're supporting me by blowing smoke up my ass. In this case, one of two things is going to happen. I'm going to get better at gymnastics, be happy with my accomplishments, even though I realize I'm not Olympic material, and I will also realize that you weren't being completely honest with me. Or, I'm going to get better at gymnastics but feel like a complete fool, because I now know I never had a chance, and you weren't being completely honest with me. In either scenario, honesty is a casualty, and now I can't believe anything you tell me. Just like Mrs. Dykman in Lesson 10, the honesty I didn't like was tough to take, but it allowed me to believe her when she was saying things I did like. If someone asks you, be honest. If they don't ask, don't answer.

People, especially nowadays, only need your honest opinion when they're ready to hear it, not when you're ready to give it. The other caveat is that honesty doesn't tolerate that secret jealousy you may harbour. If I say I want to be an Olympic gymnast, you can't say you don't think that's possible because you don't want to see me being successful at something when you don't feel successful. If this is the motivation for your opinion, you've fallen into the herd mentality and also sacrificed your honesty at the hands of your own insecurities.

Now one of three things is going to happen:

1. I'm going to give up my dream of being a gymnast. Most people think that when dreams go unattended that they just die. Dreams never really die, and when they go unattended, they turn inwards and eat you up

inside. Think about how many abandoned dreams and aspirations you have that live inside you as regrets. They float around for years, and their influence isn't usually positive.

2. The next possibility is that I get better at gymnastics, in spite of your lack of support. I'm satisfied with my accomplishments, and I think, *Humph to you for peeing on my parade.*

3. Lastly, I may get a bit better at gymnastics in spite of your lack of support, I'll be bitter about my limited progress, and I'll think, *Screw you for not believing in me, this is all your fault! If you had supported me, I could have been a contender!*

So, honesty is crucial, but brutality is not. Deliver your truth gently, like you would to a child, but deliver it you must. If you're afraid to tell someone something, it's usually because you're afraid they will be unreasonable, or that you're being unreasonable and you're afraid they'll notice. Know the difference. If you build someone up to think they can do something and they can't, the fallout can be devastating. If you hold someone back by telling them they can't do something when they can, the fallout can be devastating.

When we all work together, we can be a tidal wave, causing unimaginable destruction in our wake, or we can be a gentle swell, carrying a boat to shore. We can join together to destroy life in a furious current, or we can gently feed fields of life by sustaining crops, forests, and meadows.

I propose that we join together to build each other up and work to make the best team possible, but ultimately, the choice is yours.

THE JOURNAL:

There is a quote most often attributed to motivational speaker Jim Rohn that says, "You're the average of the five people you spend the most time with." But in a recent article by David Burkus (*The Mission*, May 23, 2018), there is some evidence to show that our circle of influence extends much further than our five closest friends. Studies show that even friends of our friends' friends can influence us, regardless of whether we've met them or not. After all, we are all connected!

Back in Lesson 1, you may have written down some things you admire about those closest to you. In this journal entry, I ask you to expand on that. Write down some of the qualities you admire most. What traits do you strive to adopt in your own journey to become the best version of you? What traits do you strive to minimize? Knowing yourself and your direction is crucial to development. As I said before, conscious people learn from happiness. They try to recreate the positive, not just avoid the negative. "Successful" people say, "Yes! That worked! I have to remember how I did that!" But most of us wait until something goes wrong and then say, "Well, I'm never doing *that* again!"

The problem with the second approach is that there are a many ways to do things wrong, and only a few ways to do them right, to align with your soul's purpose. It's like using a map or a GPS. You find where you want to be and get directions to go there. You don't find where you are now and just drive away from that point. There are too many directions away from where you are that won't get you closer to where you want to be. So, know where you are and what you're striving for. Because our circle of influence is so large, it's important to surround ourselves with groups of positive people, not just individuals.

What groups exist in your area that you could affiliate yourself with? Meditation groups? Habitat for Humanity? The Rotary Club? Your local church? Write down the names and contact numbers for a couple of groups who share your interests, skill sets, and positive outlook. Research what those groups do and where they do it. How can you participate to feed your soul? Call those people! We are all connected. Make your closest connections ones that feed and sustain your spirit. Support and be supported in ways that allow you to help each other become the best versions of yourselves. Find your team.

LESSON 20:

WHEN THE CREEK IS LOW AND BECOMES JUST A LITTLE TRICKLE, IT GIVES US A CHANCE TO REALLY NOTICE AND APPRECIATE OUR SURROUNDINGS AND THE OTHER DROPLETS TRAVELLING WITH US.

At the time of writing, Grimsby was enduring an unseasonable heat wave. There had been many days of 30C plus temperatures and no rain. The creek had formed many pools, as mentioned in Lesson 8, and there were many stretches where it barely trickled over the rocky creek bed. While these rocky stretches may not seem ideal in life, they give us unique opportunities to notice who and what is around us. We can get some valuable insight into how the members of our circle behave when conditions are not ideal. Typically, these times are more troublesome than traumatic, giving us a chance to look around if we choose to.

Often times, when our focus is monopolized by some goal or traumatic event, we will find ourselves looking *with* the people around us, not *at* the people around us. Who are they? What do you love about them? Do you have expectations of them that are more about what *you* want than who *they* are? Are some people there just because they've been there for years?

Are there people there who have gone unappreciated? Do all the people in your tribe actually deserve the space you hold for them, and do you fully appreciate and demonstrate to the ones who do? In Lesson 19, we talked about your circle and what traits you admire in your friends. Now let's go a bit deeper.

These times when things may not be going quite according to plan, but there are no real immediate threats, are a great chance to evaluate, cultivate, and appreciate your circle. We discussed in Lesson 17 that the pools give us a chance to regroup and reinvest, and we will discuss in the next lesson that the rocky patches can make the water in the creek (us) actually sparkle like diamonds. This lesson is focused a bit more outside ourselves. Our inner world is always reflected in our outer world, and what we create outside ourselves can often come as a surprise, because most of us don't practice real introspection or know ourselves in a loving fashion.

We hide the parts of ourselves that we don't like, without realizing that the parts we hide usually take a least part of our beauty into the dark with them. Then we end up with much of ourselves in shadow, hidden from us and the world. Once we realize (Lesson 1) that we are beings made of light, love and stardust, we also realize that "negative" traits we are trying to hide don't negate our beauty. These traits are often employed to act as a blind or a shield, so that people won't see our true selves, but if we can bravely acknowledge, sit with and shine some light on these defences and dark parts, gradually we gain the confidence to shine our light outwards as well.

These little slow or rocky patches give us an excellent chance to give others the benefit of the same sort of gentle exploration that we employed with the goal of being honest with ourselves. It's difficult in our present climate to navigate the line between critical judgement and assessment. We are strongly discouraged (one might even say judged!) from judging, but also encouraged to cut negative people from our circle. We give up on broken things, broken people, broken pets and broken systems.

Judgement is inherent if we are to adopt this new approach to just about everything in the modern world, but somehow, we're meant to accomplish this "pruning" of all the negative influences in our lives without judging them to be negative. It's an impossible task. We all judge. Judgement is a necessary part of life, criticism is not. In today's vernacular, the two terms are often confused. When your assessment of someone is not what they want to hear, they will often call it "judgement." When your assessment produces a conclusion they're okay with, they tend to call that "acceptance" or "support." There is judgement involved in both of those cases. If anyone decides to remove an influence from their lives, or add one, they've made a judgement. Acceptance doesn't require action. It's more like dropping the walls, opening up, and relaxing the defences and denial you have been working so hard to maintain.

Take some time to look at the people in your life. You can start with your family, for instance. When a parent isn't frustrating the heck out of you, what do you love about them? Have you told them? What about your kids? Have you taken time lately to look at who they are, as opposed to who you hope they will be? What do you love about them? Have you told them? When you compliment someone on something positive, it helps grow that part (even for your parents!), because everyone loves to be nourished and approved of. Children, especially, are such fragile souls. Ask them what they think about things and listen to their answers. Find something you like and compliment it, and that quality will grow ten-fold. Find something you admire and verbally acknowledge it, and watch out! They'll be on cloud nine and wondering how they can let more of their true selves out in public. Then you can extend the practice out to your friend circle.

Extending this practice to include your friends may or may not be easier, because presumably, you picked these people to be in your life. Sometimes, we can even have a kind of love/hate relationship with our friends. Initially, we can gravitate to people because we assess them to have qualities we think we'd also like to possess. Then, after knowing them awhile, if we are unable to become that way, but that person continues to be that way, we get angry or even hate them, *because* of the very qualities that attracted us to them in the first place.

Let's take compassion, for example. I met Freeja and immediately loved her compassion for animals, other people, the planet... You name it, she could feel for it. It's something I have wanted to work on for my personal growth, so I choose to surround myself with someone like minded. I take my cue from her, start working on my compassion, and I make some baby steps. I've read *Lessons From the Creek,* so I take a sick neighbour a casserole.

Compassion (or perhaps thoughtfulness and sensitivity) is not something I come by naturally, but I'm sure trying, with Freeja's behaviour as a guide.

Freeja and I meet for coffee a couple days later, and I'm excited to tell her my news. She's proud of me and very encouraging, so I'm feeling pretty good! Then I find out that Freeja has started an owl sanctuary in her back yard, she's going to Haiti next week to feed stray dogs, and she's started volunteering at a soup kitchen two days a week. Now I feel like a damn fool, and I become resentful of her, because I see her behaviour (which actually has nothing to do with me) as a critical judgement of my behaviour.

I end up pulling away, because Freeja is so full of herself and clearly flaunting my inadequacies at me, and what does she do? Well, she's very compassionate by nature, so she senses something's wrong with me and—you guessed it—she expresses compassion for whatever I'm going through. Now I feel even worse and riddled with guilt about how I'm treating this saint, so I pull away even more.

Freeja senses something is really wrong now, so she sends me flowers to "cheer me up" and... You get the idea. She ends up hurt, I end up bitter, and I've lost a good friend, because *I* made it a competition. Acceptance of others is so important, but acceptance of ourselves is crucial. Self-doubt doesn't just hurt you, it hurts the people around you, the same way I hurt Freeja. If I can shut my ego up for a minute and look at our interaction from her point of view, she probably wonders why it's so hard to keep friends, even when she's striving to be a caring and considerate person. She probably can't imagine what she did wrong and may feel like she shouldn't bother trying anymore. She may eventually start to doubt her value as a person, and it all started because of my insecurities.

So have a look at your friend pool. Revisit what qualities your friends have that you love, and then free yourself to love them without critically judging yourself or competing.

Look at the other people in your life as well. If you want to run a successful restaurant, talk to some successful restaurant owners. Most people love to impart little tidbits of wisdom, and you can gather those up to use when needed! Do the same for character traits. If you have people in your life about whom you struggle to find things you love, maybe you might want to redirect your attention. Remember that energy follows focus, so if you really can't find qualities you admire to focus on, maybe it's time to re-evaluate their place in your circle. You don't have to arbitrarily cut anyone out of your life, but you can prioritize who you make space and time for. People tend to display their true colours during the troublesome times, so have a look at your tribe, and when they show you who they are, believe them.

THE JOURNAL:

As with all of the journal entries, this is for your eyes only, so be honest. Write a list of your people. Write down what you love about them. If you're struggling to decide whether to give someone space, write down a list of pros and cons. This is not a "thought" list. You have to write it down. When it comes to people we think we love, we often downplay unpleasant past experiences, so you may be surprised at the results after you review and write down all the "negative" points. If the negatives outweigh the positives, take a bit of a step back and redirect your attention. You can either focus on their positive qualities if you want to maintain a relationship with them, or you can notice, appreciate and focus on fellow water droplets who add value to your life. In either case, your attention and appreciation will add value to their lives, and then everyone grows.

LESSON 21:

THE CREEK REFLECTS THE SUNLIGHT BEST
WHEN IT GOES OVER SOME ROCKS.

IT IS DURING THOSE ROCKY PARTS OF THE CREEK'S
JOURNEY THAT THE WATER DROPLETS SPARKLE
AND LOOK LIKE DIAMONDS IN THE SUN.

We have probably all heard sayings and songs that encourage us to shine like diamonds because each of us is like one of those multi-faceted, precious gems. I couldn't agree more, but what most people forget is that the only way coal transforms into a diamond is by undergoing tremendous heat and pressure. Many motivational quotes suggest that life's trials and tribulations will produce the same results for us, and these euphemisms used to frustrate me to no end. I could sometimes recognize that the hard times I was experiencing might make me a better person eventually, but how was I supposed to get through it right now? The answer? Hold on! Don't give up! Don't expend your energy thinking about how hard it is, thinking that you have a choice to go through it, or feeling sorry for yourself. It *is* hard, and I'm not saying that focusing on how you're going to do this, how awesome you're going to feel when it's over because you're proud you got through it without compromising your morals, and how great your circle is will make it easy (although it just might!). What I'm saying is that a focus on those positive and proactive aspects *will* get you through this, and you'll sparkle like a diamond while you're doing it!

It is a well-known fact that hard times often have a habit of pulling people together, but hard times can also help you pull *yourself* together. We talked about stress in Lesson 2, and many of us actually perform better under pressure. Pressure can help remove the illusion of choice, and as long as we don't artificially add to it, help raise the quality of our performance. When we manage the pressure in a responsible fashion, we can find our "flow state" and often surprise ourselves with what we are capable of.

When my ex-husband and I had our running groups, one of the best-selling features was the group atmosphere. Whether people are competitive or not, there's a (healthy) sense of responsibility when you're part of a group to show up and perform. We tried not to let anyone push their limitations to the point of injury, but stepping a bit out of your comfort zone is a good thing. Running with a couple of people who are a bit faster, or can run a bit longer without stopping, almost always improves a person's performance. So does consistent practice. The runners who showed up three times a week, every week, noticed real improvements.

In addition, especially for new runners, we didn't accept fear as a valid reason to not start running. We knew that anyone was capable of running, so convincing fearful people they could do it was where our work came in. We started them out slowly, we encouraged, and then we got to watch as so many people exceeded their own expectations. They broke free of their self-limiting beliefs and sparkled like diamonds.

We generally keep ourselves in a much smaller box (one might even say cage) than we need to. A little well-placed pressure can break down the barriers that are meant to keep us so safe that we sacrifice experience. We don't tend to push ourselves as much as life or other people push us, because of fear and because it can be uncomfortable. We've all heard the sayings that encourage us to get out of our comfort zone, but what does that really mean?

I think many people feel getting out of your comfort zone means that we should do something wild and adventurous, like skydiving or travelling to an exotic destination. What I don't think people realize is that when we have lived much of our lives in abusive relationships or toxic situations, embarking on a healthy approach can really push our limits, thereby making us quite uncomfortable. There's an illusion that being healthy, whether that means in a relationship, physically, or emotionally, is easy because it's the right thing to do.

Change, even if it's positive change, isn't easy. It's scary. It's different. And it can feel awful at first, because it's not what you're used to. Doing a detox after you've been eating crap for a long time will make you feel sick for a few days while your body dumps out all the garbage that's accumulated. Being in a giving relationship can feel dull or even completely wrong if you've gotten used to, or even embraced, having the life sucked out of you by takers in your past. The adrenaline produced by drama can be as addicting as it is damaging. Slipping back into habitual behaviours of suspicion and defensiveness can alienate the wonderful person you had been waiting for, because they feel so bad when you are unable to trust them.

Just remember that change is uncomfortable, but it's the only way to get different results, so keep going. The transition between leaving old habits and negative influences behind and the creation of new habits and positive connections, can feel eternal and desolate. Keep going. Feeling fantastic, having the relationship you want, and being healthy is waiting for you just outside your comfort zone. You don't have to jump out of a plane to get there, you just have to endure a bit of discomfort.

I can't remember how many people told me I was much better off without my ex-husband when he left. I was inclined to agree, but that certainly didn't make the hurt stop immediately. It didn't even make me feel a whole lot better, and it didn't make the painful process of healing any less painful. What positive thoughts like that did do, was help me soldier on, even though it was hard as hell. Positive thoughts like that encouraged me to have faith that I would not always hurt this much, without trying to trivialize the pain I was feeling at that moment.

I can't emphasize this part of your personal growth enough, and many people don't talk about it. There is a common misconception that spiritual awakening or enlightenment is some blissful process, like nirvana or paradise, where nothing hurts, nothing ruffles your feathers, and all your friends start treating you like you're the Dalai Lama. What it really looks like is more like a cat that has just fallen into a full bathtub scrambling to get out while its owners look on, laughing and trying to catch the whole thing on video, so they can post it on YouTube.

As I endeavoured to recover from the rather ungainly end of my twenty-year relationship, I struggled to keep moving forward. I crawled under an emotional rock on many days. I lost some friends but found that the good ones continued to reach out to me when they knew I was so far in a hole that I couldn't reach out to them. When things finally started getting better, they started to fall apart. People who had never been through a similar experience, critically judged my recovery. The more I grew and invested love and care into myself, the more people I seemed to lose.

Intellectually, I knew that you can't fill a cup that's already full, and the retreat of negative influences would create room that positive things could eventually fill, but how could I navigate the space in between? Each time someone would exit, by their choice or mine, I would do some ruthless self-examination just to make sure I wasn't acting like an asshole. I would ask a couple of people I trusted to tell me the truth if I was, in fact, behaving badly. If the consensus was not-asshole, I would ask the Universe what I was supposed to learn, forgive, and let go. If the consensus was yes-asshole, I would spend some time in reflection trying to figure out why I had opted for that approach or response. I would ask the Universe what I was supposed to learn, forgive (myself) and let go. Then I did my best to continue growing and shining.

This time was certainly a rocky patch in my journey. In life, we do sometimes have a choice of when you go through these times and how. Whether or not you go through them is not our choice. I lost people I loved, who I never thought I'd lose. I lost them when I didn't have anyone else waiting in the wings. I was leaving a lifestyle that I had cultivated for years, unable to see what was ahead. Having at least one good friend was key. Faith that I was moving in the right direction toward something better was key. Faith in the Universal law that states you can't keep doing the right thing and continue getting the wrong thing was key. Gratitude for and focus on the good things was key. Remembering that I could always choose to take the high road was key. The rocky patch may not be your choice, but whether or not you sparkle certainly is!

THE JOURNAL:

If you've picked this book up, you're probably on the road to personal growth. In my experience, the biggest impediment to this pursuit is what we try to bring with us from our past. We try to create a new environment from the same old us. Memories can elicit the same chemical reactions in your body as an actual event can. Anchors to our past aren't always negative in appearance. Just because you love someone doesn't mean you should try and bring them along on your journey. Letting go of someone doesn't mean giving up on them, it just means you accept that you may no longer be in the same place. You can't grow another person. You can't make someone listen. You can't love them enough to save them, especially if they don't want to save themselves, and rescuing prevents healing.

What are you trying to bring with you on your journey? Habits? People? Beliefs? Write a list. Write a few lines about each item on the list and what each one means to you. Spend some time in contemplation of each item, with the intention of deciding whether your attachment is holding you back. I repeat, this is not about giving up, it's about recognizing who or what you may be trying to control, and how letting go of that desire or compulsion can set you free to sparkle.

When you come up with something you feel you are ready to let go, you can write it on a piece of paper and burn it. You can close your eyes and picture yourself trying to drag an anchor that's been tied around your waist. Picture how difficult it is to drag this heavy, awkward thing along uneven ground or a sandy beach. When you're ready, picture yourself cutting it free and leaving it behind. Watch as it disintegrates in the sun or rain or waves and as the remaining dust ends up being blown away by the wind or washed away in the ocean. Now it's really gone! Hard times and recovery are never easy and hardly ever pretty, but you can shine by enduring the heat and pressure of a challenging situation, freeing yourself from unhealthy attachments to your past and choosing to move forward.

LESSON 22:

THE WATER LEVELS IN THE CREEK CAN VARY GREATLY FROM DAY TO DAY, WEEK TO WEEK, AND SEASON TO SEASON.

THESE CONDITIONS CAN CAUSE SUBTLE CHANGES IN THE CREEK'S PATH, THE CREEK BOTTOM, AND THE CREEK'S BANKS, BUT THE CREEK ALWAYS RECOVERS ... AND SO CAN YOU.

This lesson is about resilience and the crucial role resilience plays in recovery, growth, and inner peace. Peace is something I hear many people talking about lately. There are so many talking about eliminating people, things and drama from their lives to maintain peace. It's like they think peace is something you create outside to protect your equilibrium inside. In truth, creating a rock solid, unshakeable equilibrium inside means you don't have to worry about what happens outside, and as we know by now, you can't always control what happens there anyway. Some call it living in joy, living in the moment or detachment, but whatever you call it, it is the only way of being free to offer ourselves to this experience rather than protecting ourselves from it. That protection can become a cage in a heartbeat, and that's fear, not peace at all.

So, the trick is to gain unshakeable personal peace and not let any discomfort unseat that. "How do we do that?" you may ask...

I've employed several methods of "peace keeping" throughout my life, some more effective than others. Drinking alcohol and eating chips didn't work. I tried each on its own, and both in tandem (many times, just to make sure). Didn't work! I took Tai Chi for a while and loved it. I tried yoga. Didn't love it. Running worked for many years, but not everyone is up to the physical component, so walking (especially in nature) can be a better strategy. Recently, I've found it very helpful to meditate, and at the suggestion of my stepson, chanting has also been very beneficial. Both of these approaches are great, because you don't have to attend a class (though there are many available if you prefer), there are lots of resources online, and you can do both in the comfort of your own home.

It's very difficult for most of us to be still these days. Oh sure, you can plop on the couch with a glass of wine after a long day at work and watch some TV, but this is numbness, not stillness. Many of us don't like the idea of spending quiet time by ourselves all that much, because we don't actually like our own company all that much. Hopefully, if you've reread some of the other lessons and your journal entries, you now realize there are plenty of things to like about you. Take ten or fifteen minutes and sit by yourself with no disruptions. Once you get past the feeling that you really should be doing something else, you'll come to really enjoy that time.

Thoughts may come into your head, but you just usher them right back out again. Don't get into a fight by trying to block them, just notice, tell your mind you'll think about each thought a bit later, and be still. Once you carve out one ten or fifteen-minute space in your day for a few days in a row, try fitting in a second one. Morning and evening are great times to meditate, and if you sit up during your evening session in particular, so you don't fall asleep, after a couple nights you'll find it really helps when you do go to sleep. Just a bit of time, whether you decide on meditation, yoga, or beekeeping, will actually help all through the day. You will develop some inner peace to help handle the outer pressure.

It also helps to remember the "good thing, bad thing ... who knows?" proverb from Lesson 2. An event that appears catastrophic today may end up being an incredible stroke of good luck. We live in a world of instant gratification, but the Universe works on the principle of process. Western culture is one of superlatives, yet the Universe speaks in subtleties. Events in our lives only have influence on our demeanour when we assign a label of positive or negative. When something you think of as awful happens, try to take a mental step back and see if you can see another way to look at it that feels more positive. Experiencing a power outage is a simple example of how you can shift your thinking. You can focus on the fact that you can't watch your usual TV sitcom line-up and get upset about that, or you can focus on what you can do to make it fun. Lighting candles, looking at the night sky without all the light pollution and roasting hotdogs over a backyard bonfire with your kids and the neighbours, are all things that can cultivate new forms of gratitude and joy. You just have to shift your perception.

Thirdly, having a goal is a great way to stay on track, as discussed in Lesson 9. As long as you don't become too attached or inflexible regarding the final outcome, you can be open to minor shifts or changes that may produce a better result. Having a dream, creating a vision board, and setting an intention are all effective tools to help you reach your goal. Focusing on the individual steps necessary to get you to the final accomplishment can be very helpful in maintaining your resilience and daily dedication. Break your big goal down into bite-sized pieces and then focus on what you need to do right now. As you work away at each step, enjoy the process. Appreciate that you are working on your dream and be grateful for what you are doing this minute. Don't let the fact that you haven't yet reached your goal ruin the joy that comes from the process of progress.

Finally, living in the moment is a very effective way of escaping the anxiety associated with worrying about the future, and the depression that can come from reliving the past. As with appreciating the process involved in achieving your goals, stop during your hectic days and appreciate where you are right now. There are apps, reminders on your Fitbit, and lots of literature on mindfulness, so incorporate whatever works for you into your daily routine. Even a little deep breathing for two minutes can help immensely when you just need to centre yourself. It's a very manageable bit of quiet peace (not like trying to carve out time and sit down to 15-30 minutes of meditation), and nothing that you have or don't have, worries, bills, a million dollars, makes any difference in this two minutes. As Eckhart Tolle asks in his book, *The Power of Now*, "If not this, then what?"

You can't, and shouldn't, eliminate pressure from your life. It's what pushes you towards growth and greatness. Handling the pressure from a position of peace encourages growth instead of stress. Inner peace allows you to thrive instead of just survive. Creating this solid base of unshakeable peace and resilience means that, no matter how the water levels rise or fall, you will find your way back to centre faster and with the wisdom gained from experience.

THE JOURNAL:

If you didn't already have a goal, think about something you'd like to achieve. When you've decided on something, break it down into steps (daily, weekly, monthly if need be) and then remember to enjoy each of those steps. Commit to write a couple lines in your journal every day about what you accomplished today in the process of realizing your goal and how awesome it was!

Find a meditation app, a mindfulness app, or a class that you feel you can devote the needed time to. You're important, so give yourself some valuable, soul-nourishing attention. You deserve it! Set a reminder on your phone so you can give yourself at least two minutes of stillness a few times a day.

Lastly, recall a time in your life when something happened that you labelled as horrible actually turned out to be positive. Maybe you lost a job and ended up with a much better one that you loved. Maybe you missed out on renting a great apartment only to find one the next day that was much better. These events happen all the time. We just tend to forget. You can use your past experiences to help you have faith, and look at things a little differently the next time something "bad" happens. This faith, change in perspective and solid inner peace will keep you from plummeting to the depths of despair in reaction to events in your outer world. It's much easier to recover when you haven't been helplessly tossed around on an ocean of emotion, and recover, you will!

LESSON 23:

MOST OF US FEEL HEARING THE SOUND OF A BABBLING BROOK OR LISTENING TO WAVES GENTLY LAPPING UP ON SHORE CAN BE VERY CALMING.

YOU TOO CAN IMPART PEACE TO THOSE AROUND YOU WHEN YOU ARE AT PEACE. IT'S CONTAGIOUS!

The message here is twofold:

1. We discussed in Lesson 19, that it's important to consider who you surround yourself with. Because we are all connected, we feel energy from the people around us. If we also happen to be empathic, we feel the energy a *lot* more.
I'm sure we all know those people who make us anxious just by being around them. In her book, *The Artist's Way,* Julia Cameron refers to these people as "crazy makers." This, and more recently, the term narcissistic personality disorder (NPD) are both used to describe similar types of people. These people attempt to manipulate people and situations in their own favour. It takes a pretty strong core of personal peace

to resist being shaken by these whirlwinds of contrived, self-serving anxiety and drama. Our attempts to ignore these energy vampires and their antics, can often lead us into the shadowy realm of indifference. We tell ourselves, "They can knock themselves out! See if I care!" or "Zero f*#ks given!" These are not places we want to go either. Pointedly not caring about anyone else has helped no one ever. So, you can care about self-absorbed Mr. or Mrs. Ants-in-their-pants, while not letting their behaviour disrespect you or disrupt your peace, because you also care about you.

This is not about using the premise of being hurt or offended solely to manipulate someone else's behaviour. Being offended doesn't mean you're right. The tactics of feigned sensitivity and indignation are used all too often. Generally, these tactics are employed to try and remove our permission for people to speak their truth, especially when we don't like their truth, or to manipulate others before they can manipulate us. This is about dealing with authentic hurt and boundaries while maintaining your inner peace.

At first, keeping your own peace is difficult, but you must be vigilant. If you meet or already know someone who has you wanting a couple shots of tequila and a smoke after talking to them for half an hour, don't talk to them for half an hour. Centre yourself in your peace (this is where those two-minute mindfulness apps can come in handy) and talk to them for fifteen minutes instead. Then hang up the phone or walk away and centre yourself in your peace again. Pat yourself on the back for not losing your cool and controlling the only thing you can: your reaction. You'll notice a difference and so will they.

All you need to do is as much as you feel okay with, so you have no regrets. This is the best you can do. You staying calm will either help calm them or send a message that you will not be manipulated out of your state of calm. Win/win! If you have people in your life who antagonize you, and you don't want to just walk away from them, let them know gently, with love. There is a chance that they may not actually realize their behaviour makes you want to stick a fork in your eye. If you can think about what you love about them while you're telling them what bugs you, it will come from a place of love. If your concerns are real, tell them from your heart, like you're talking (gently, not condescendingly) to a child. If they really didn't know that what they did or said bothered you, and you tell them with love, you'll likely get a response like "Oh my gosh! I had no idea! I'm so sorry!" Then you can reassure them, explain if you want to (you certainly don't have to!), and express your true appreciation for being heard. If you're mad when you tell them, they will feel that whether they're empathic or not. They'll be much more likely to get defensive and less likely to hear you and respond in a positive manner. If you adopt the position of martyr/victim because you feel they hurt you, you'll push them into the persecutor roll and you'll likely get a response that involves some eye rolling and criticism for being so sensitive.

If you can say, out of love, something like "I have so much fun with you, and I enjoy our time together, so I just want to tell you that it bothers me when you call me dumbass. You may be joking, but it bugs me. Could you please stop doing that?" It's so much better than saying something like "Oh yeah? Well, *you're* a dumbass! Don't like it, eh? So, *stop* calling me that!" or "I can't believe you call me that! It's abusive and hurtful! How could you?" The first option is most likely to get a positive result. You avoid the angry "blow out" (because you're not bottling stuff up inside), and you avoid intentionally inflicting guilt (because you're just being authentic, not manipulating). Manipulation and holding things in aren't good for you, and both tactics significantly reduce the chance of a positive resolution. If you've told them that something they say or do hurts your feelings or upsets you, you've given them the chance to change by informing them that their words or actions hurt you. If, at this point, they refuse to change, you need to change. It's that simple.

You can set some boundaries for your interactions (I'll only see them when there's a group of us). You can limit your time with them. You can walk away when they say or do whatever bothers you (it might be good to tell them what you're doing in this case; "I'm walking away from you right now, because you called me a dumb blonde and I've told you that bothers me, so I'm leaving. I'll talk to you later). You can refuse to answer them when they address you in a derogatory manner, etc.

What you cannot do is continue to tolerate the behaviour and then bitch about how the other person isn't changing. You aren't changing either, and they're not the one who's bothered by their behaviour, you are. You have the power to set rules as to how you are treated and the responsibility to hold up those boundaries. If you give that power away, you don't get to criticize what someone else does with it.

2. Figure out how to establish your own inner peace. We touched on this in Lesson 22, but you really need to find what makes you peaceful and spread that around. I mentioned that meditation and chanting help me a great deal, but this is a very personal thing. For you, painting might work, or writing, or one of those adult colouring books, or running, or yoga. Whatever re-establishes your calm is great! If counting to ten and taking a couple of deep breaths are enough to keep you from turning into a whirling dervish, fantastic! Never compromise your peace, but always be willing to share it. If people ask what you've been doing, tell them. If you've been taking a class and a friend expresses an interest, invite them along to the next one. Share your strategies with those who take a real interest, so they can not only find their own peace, but also share with their friends and family. The more peace we develop and share, the better.

Hurt people hurt people, so if someone is trying to hurt you on purpose, chances are they're in a lot of pain themselves. If they can create some peace, and you can help, you also help all the other people who they might be trying to hurt. Gandhi said, "Be the change you wish to see in the world." This is a great way of doing that from your little corner!

THE JOURNAL:

Do you have "crazy-makers" or narcissists in your life? That's actually a trick question. We all do! Write down a name or two (or more!) in your journal. Can you establish some boundaries with some or all of these people? What could you say, out of love, to teach them how you expect to be treated?

Once you have established and practiced some strategies for promoting your inner peace, how can you share? Sometimes sharing your vulnerability can provide a comfortable space for someone else to be vulnerable also. It's scary, but you can still try it. The worst that will happen is that someone scoffs or laughs, and then you get to practice maintaining your inner peace. If you offer out of love and someone refuses, snickers or mocks you, it just means that they're not ready. It does not mean your vulnerability makes you less of a person.

I will add a caveat at this point: There are some people who you will need to walk away from. Many narcissists will only interact with you to manipulate you, and if you engage in a relationship with these people, you are enabling, not helping. It is easy to lose your way, because they are expert at their craft and target individuals who want to help. When you are helping someone create their own peace, there will only be positive feelings. If at any time someone makes you feel empty or used (even if they also make you feel great sometimes), there is something wrong in that relationship. Love gives and multiplies by having been given. Manipulation costs the person being manipulated, and when they say stop, or are depleted, the manipulator will move on to the next target. I always promote working to make our world a better place because we are all connected, but this is one of the very few times that the only way out is by walking away.

LESSON 24:

GIVEN A CHOICE, THE CREEK WILL TAKE
THE PATH OF LEAST RESISTANCE.

IF THE CREEK CONTINUES ON THIS PATH FOR LONG ENOUGH,
THE ROUTE THAT IT ERODES BECOMES DEEPER AND DEEPER.

EVENTUALLY THE CREEK BED BECOMES INESCAPABLE
WITHOUT A TRAUMATIC EVENT SUCH AS A
FLOOD OR TORRENTIAL DOWNPOUR.

We all have habits that we would like to give up. I sometimes feel like I drink too much, but working in the service industry for so long, it has been a hard habit to break. Drinking has also become an integral part of the western social structure, fuelled by clever advertising and peer pressure. It's summer in Niagara right now, so events at local wineries and backyard barbecues make drinking alcohol almost a given. When I meet someone who doesn't drink, it's usually because they never have, or they were addicted at some point. Even alcoholics can stop for a designated time, but if you just say, "Stop drinking indefinitely," that's when people, alcoholics and non-alcoholics alike, tend to struggle. The problem is fear of heading into the unknown by making a lasting change, and this is only partly due to the addiction piece.

Changing is hard work, whether it's positive or not. In Lesson 21, we talked about how uncomfortable it can be. The danger in not changing is how entrenched we can become in the status quo. The creek will follow the course it has etched out in the land it runs over, even if that course is not the most direct route. It will continue until it carves a deeper and deeper bed, like the Grand Canyon. After a point, it might be impossible, or at least very difficult, to change.

As water droplets, we tend to go with the flow and follow our fellow water droplets down the path of least resistance. Even when it may not be the best path for our own experience, we follow along because we're already going that way and our friends are going that way too. Often, we feel helpless to get out of that rut we are in, but whatever you are not changing, you are choosing. Our power lies in our ability to choose. We always have choice, but the choices we want to make are not always easy. When we give up the notion that what's best for us should be easy, then, and only then, can we make progress. Waiting can make taking action much harder than it has to be. Most of us wait to make a choice until at least one of our options is particularly distasteful, but you don't have to.

If you wait until there is a flood, as described in Lesson 2, the choice can become obvious, but it might still be painful. Pain can be a great motivator, but it encourages you to run from the problem, not to the solution. Running *from* requires us to direct our attention to our past, rather than directing our attention to doing what we need to do in the *present* to create the best possible future. You can run away from something in an infinite number of directions, while creating the future we want requires us to focus on one direction: to.

Until recently, I too found it easier to detach and adopt the "good thing, bad thing ... who knows?" attitude when I was in pain. In happiness, I would still become earthbound and complacent, like "Okay, this is how it's supposed to be, so I can just relax and enjoy." I didn't take the time to learn when I was in a pool before a rocky bit (Lesson 17), and I tended to rest on my laurels. That complacency pulled me down and away from my higher self and my personal growth. I suppose that's why I've had more sorrow than happiness in my life. I chose sorrow to be the catalyst for my desire to learn, so pain and fear were the methods the Universe employed to teach me. That was my choice. Now I choose to learn from happiness and joy, repeating the right things, not just avoiding the painful things, so the Universe can use more positive and pleasant events for my education. Again, it is and always has been my choice.

Be wary of becoming complacent. Be wary of "the devil you know is better than the one you don't" attitude. Be wary of staying in your box because it's comfortable. Great risk offers the potential of great reward, so when contemplating a change, ask yourself, "What's the worst that could happen?" Then think about the best that could happen. Chances are that the best is even better than you can imagine, but nothing changes until you start to change things. You are responsible for getting the ball rolling, and there's no time like the present to start. If jumping out of the rut scares us, it's generally because we tend to imagine the worst possible outcome from making that change. That's your ego using fear to support your complacency and maintain the "comfortable" status quo. In truth, the Universe will recognize your efforts to grow, and every small step forward will be rewarded. That still won't make change easy, but it will show you that your efforts are being recognized and encouraged. To receive conformation, you just have to choose to look for it, instead of focusing on how uncomfortable you are.

THE JOURNAL:

Write down all the details you can about what your best life would look like if nothing stood in your way. Picture what your day-to-day existence would be like if you were living the life of your dreams. Look at your life now and write down everything you do on a day-to-day basis. Most of us are pretty habitual. This is your creek bed (the path of least resistance), which gets deeper and deeper the longer it goes unchanged. This is not about money; it's more about feelings. Most of us want to be happy, but what will help us achieve that? Having a million dollars in the bank won't make you happy if you're not right now, and you don't change anything. If you want money, what are you hoping it will do for you? If you want better health, what are you hoping that will do for you? If you're hoping money or health might get you more freedom, focus on the freedom, and the money and better health will come.

Now compare your lists. What are you doing now that is not coherent with the life that you want? What attitudes do you have now, that perpetuate your rut? I once saw a Facebook meme that said, "Visualize the life that want and don't do anything that isn't that." It's that simple. When you visualize the life you want, start feeling the way think you will feel when you are in that life, and doing the things that you will do when you're in that life, the Universe responds by aligning with your intentions. Live more like you have the life you want, and the Universe will respond by delivering aspects that align with the energy you're emitting. Positive actions create positive reactions and we manifest from the energy of who we're becoming, not from what we're wishing for.

So, figure out what positive actions you can take, but don't beat yourself up if you have negative thoughts; just change them when you notice them. If you start feeling sorry for yourself, notice and then change those thoughts to thoughts of how happy you're going to be when the life that you want manifests. Your ego will tell you that your dreams are stupid and they'll never happen. Dream anyway. Think of visualization like you're watching a movie or TV show. It's inspirational and personal and as long as your visualization inspires you to make one small step in the right direction every day, every day you're closer to making that dream a reality. Don't focus on trying to get rid of the negative thoughts, as that directs your energy their way. Just focus on adding positive ones. The negative thoughts will fall off when there's no longer room for them in your positive mental environment. It's a skill and will take some practice, but the only way things change is when you choose to change them.

LESSON 25:

HOW WE ARE NOT LIKE THE CREEK.

LIFE IS NOT JUST ABOUT GETTING TO A CERTAIN POINT FROM WHERE WE ARE NOW; IT'S ABOUT THE JOURNEY WE TRAVEL FROM WHERE WE'VE STARTED.

IT'S NOT JUST ABOUT REACHING OR ACHIEVING A GOAL; IT'S ABOUT THE PROCESS OF LIVING AND LEARNING.

GOALS PROVIDE US WITH A DIRECTION, NOT AN ALL-OR-NOTHING TARGET THAT NEEDS TO BE HIT DIRECTLY IN THE CENTRE.

This is a little bit "tortoise and the hare" and a little bit "the first can end up last and vice versa." We all have our journey, and some of us may seem farther ahead at times because we had a head start at the beginning of this particular chapter. Some of us may have had a few more hurdles to navigate and so we've taken a more circuitous route. When you look at your life, you see one little section, which is where you are right now. Same when you look at someone else's little section. You don't know what happened in their previous sections, so it's a bit ridiculous to compare yourself to those people based on the only little section you can see from your little section. Life is so much more than the section you can see right now, so don't compare, just be present.

Western society has reached an interesting crossroads, where we deny any healthy sort of competition for our young people (everyone gets a medal because we're all winners, and it's easier for us not to have to deal with our children's disappointment), and yet we have removed any semblance of that same "humanitarianism" from the adult work place. It's really no wonder that our young people enter the workforce with big attitudes and unrealistic expectations.

For adults, our society is all about money and power. It's not about loyalty, ability, wisdom, and definitely *not* about compassion. We refuse to criticize our children (even when they need it) because we don't want to offend their delicate sensitivities, but we dress them in clothes made by children working in sweatshops who are beaten if they don't sew fast enough. Our world has become so polarized (it's *us* and *them*, no matter who "them" is), and we don't care about that disparity as long as we feel we're on the rich or "right" side. People don't realize that being rich, when so many people are poor, makes us more miserable than the poor people we're so afraid of becoming. When we truly care for (not just about) people, we fill our own cups also, because we are all connected. When we truly respect and are respected, then and only then, do we find true joy.

We hear the words "life is a journey" just about every day. It's in literature, on social media, on talk shows, and in countless quotes, but what does it mean? What call to action does that saying imply? To me, it means doing your best every minute of every day. Your best today may not be your best of yesterday, and it may not be your best of tomorrow, but it doesn't matter … and we cheat ourselves when we try to compare or compete. Pay attention right here, right now, and do whatever doing your best looks like in this moment. This is the little section where you are, so be here! Not five minutes from now, not when you lose ten pounds, not five years ago, not when you finish school, not "I'll start on Monday," and not when the person with you finishes what they're saying, so you can finally talk. *Right here!* Then you never have to feel guilty later on, because you half-assed something now. You did your best, and as a consequence, you get the absolute most out of every step of your journey and a clear conscience, to boot. Then your sections add up to a great story and an unshakeable sense of peace and self satisfaction.

I've said that the creek moves with relentless forward motion, and that I use that saying as an ultra-marathon mantra. Every race is a culmination of a *lot* of work, yes, but also a lot of rest. The stop, rest, and listen part of our journey is just as important as the training and work. If the training was the only part that mattered, we'd feel better at the end of a race than we did at the beginning. It's when we work, then rest, then work again, then rest that we get the real benefits of our training.

Luckily, we are not dragged or driven along by forces beyond our control like the water in the creek. We control and create our journey. Read that again. *We control and create our journey.* The path may be somewhat predetermined, but the journey is entirely up to us. Remember: Decision equals thought, choice equals action, and karma equals reaction. We are in the driver's seat of our bodies, minds, and consciousness. If you have a detrimental thought, you *can* stop thinking it, or change it, given the right tools. If you don't like what's happening around you, you *can* be the change.

As I said earlier, we live and we learn. If we just exist, we learn too, it just takes longer and sometimes the Universe has to step in with a nudge. I can't stress this enough, because so many people feel powerless in their lives. We have power over ourselves!! You can't make someone else change, but you can change. You can't make someone else love you, but you can choose to love yourself. You can't change many things in nature, but you can choose to learn and work with nature.

It all comes back to the questions you ask, and how you can use those questions to start training your mind. Ask the right questions. If you get the answer, listen, even if it's one you don't think you like. Choose your journey instead of agreeing to get swept along. If you give others blame, you also give them power over you, and that trade-off is never a good one. It feels fantastic when you have the good fortune to meet someone who genuinely cares about you, but even they can't do that as well as you can.

When you're in the driver's seat, you get to choose where you go, how fast you get there, and whether you want to roll the windows down or not. Take the wheel, friends!

THE JOURNAL:

This is a great opportunity to think about longer term goals. Where would you like to be in six months? A year? Two years?

If you haven't already, break these big goals down into bite-size pieces. What has to happen every month to achieve my six-month goal? Then break down each month's goals into weekly to-do lists. I even break things down to daily lists, because I love crossing things off every day. After you have your plan mapped out, focus on the process. You don't have to forget about your big goal, but you don't want to trip over a crack in the sidewalk while you're looking at the hill on the next block. Do what you need to do today, based on your plan, and enjoy the process you know is going to get you to your big goal. Visualising what you want, acting like you already have it, and being grateful are key aspects of successful manifestation, but you also need to focus on where you are right now. Try something new. Make changes. Change your perspective. If something doesn't work, you can change it tomorrow. You command every day of your life. Feel the empowerment that comes with mapping out your destiny and choosing to do what you need to do today, to get there tomorrow and be grateful.

FINAL SENTIMENTS FROM THE CREEK

I love flying. A short time ago, on a training flight for my helicopter pilot's licence, my instructor and I were flying over a field that was bordered by a forest. As we neared the tree line, a pair of bald eagles took to the air below us. Watching them soar while flying above them was a fascinating change of vantage point. I have watched many hawks and eagles soar effortlessly above me while I was walking or hiking, but seeing them from above offered a whole new experience.

Often times, I see various creeks and rivers from this same aerial vantage point and marvel at how they meander through the countryside. Creeks and rivers very seldom take the most direct route to the body of water where their journey will culminate, and it's interesting to see the turns and rapids that make up their paths. If we could look at an overview of our life's journey the same way we can see the path of a creek from the air, imagine what changes we would make. We would most certainly avoid some of the "detours" that our lives appear to have taken. It's easy to think that avoiding some of our experiences would have saved us from pain and heartache, but that avoidance would have also left us going forward without the experience and lessons that those switchbacks and rocky parts taught us.

This is not a new concept, but it's one that is important to living in the moment. We humans treat time as a linear phenomenon, and because of this, it is impossible for us to see into our future. This is a good thing and an imperative part of the human experience. Faith is crucial when we can't understand or don't like what is happening in our present. Detachment and resilience make it a bit easier to understand that the knowledge we're gaining from experiencing what we're going through now, may be very useful to us in the future. Faith steps in again when we can't imagine how that will happen.

It has been said that everything we need to know can be learned by watching nature, and after having watched the creek for so long, I am inclined to agree. Humanity has attempted to remove and disassociate itself from nature through our technological "advances" and our arrogance. What recent history has demonstrated is that our attempts to operate in ways that violate the laws of nature have been wholly unsuccessful. We've encountered so many issues unique to our species, not because of our advanced intelligence, but because of our lack of foresight and selfish exploitation of the world around us. We use up resources, including friends and family, unable (or at least unwilling) to see that this behaviour is not sustainable.

Western society embraces a "more is better" philosophy, which encourages hoarding and as a consequence, is killing us and our planet. The minimalist movement has grown in response to the damage caused by our capitalist culture. Both these approaches focus on conservation rather than feeding what we want to see grow. This may sound like it's about climate change and environmental issues, but these are just symptoms of a greater problem. We have adopted a similar exploitative attitude in our personal world as well.

Our society has become all take and give-to-get, and this is not how nature works. The need to win, have more than everybody else, and be better than everybody else is born out of insecurity. We doubt our abilities and our worth in the system that is modern humanity. When we have these feelings, we doubt ourselves instead of doubting the validity of the system. We try to fix ourselves when it's the system that's broken. The atmosphere of competition that we've created fosters jealousy, insecurity, fear, conservation and elitism, not love.

Contrary to popular belief, nature actually operates on the basis of encouragement, support, cooperation, and mutual aid. Ant colonies and beehives are obvious examples of this type of teamwork, where everyone has a job and each member's role is just as important for the well-being of the colony or hive as any other's. They help each other. They invest. They don't hoard resources that they will never need just to have them. They don't go without when they don't need to go without, because they don't have contempt for what Mother Nature provides. Big cats kill elk or gnus to eat, not to show the other big cats that they're better than them. They also enjoy the opportunities presented when presented them, knowing that there may be times of scarcity in the future.

If you compete with someone, you may be better at the task than them, but is that as good as you can be? Or just as good as you need to be to beat them? Going toward being your best will always get you further than running away from losing to someone else. Love and encouragement will always get you further than the fear of being the person behind you. On the other side of that, what happens to the person behind you? We rarely give accolades to the runners up. If they did their best, while the winners didn't, who really deserves our respect and admiration? What the runners-up are usually left with are feelings of inadequacy and shame.

A society where everyone who isn't number one feels unworthy is not a healthy society. When we reserve our attention for those who accomplish "great" things (regardless of what they're actually capable of), we leave 99 percent of our brothers and sisters feeling poorly about themselves. The current approach of giving everyone a medal is patronizing and disempowering.

"Here's a reward for sucking at soccer, but I'm not going to take the time to find out what you don't suck at."

At worst, most kids are rewarded for not doing well, and at best, they feel invisible when they are doing well. How can a race of beings succeed and grow if the vast majority of that race feels defeated, discouraged, and discarded? The answer? It can't. The majority of humanity lacks validation and acceptance. This creates feelings of isolation and emptiness, which manifest in various ways. The exponential growth rate of cases of mental illness and discoveries of new and virulent physical diseases are just two indications of the spiritual state of the disenfranchised.

It is exactly here where love and acceptance need to enter the picture. We are all connected, and when so many are feeling invisible and uncared for, it cannot help but affect us all. Loving yourself first is a concept that's thrown around these days like rice at a wedding. The intent, in many cases, is to replace the love we have been seeking from others with self-love, so we don't need anyone else. That idea isn't completely wrong, but it's a little misguided. Loving and respecting yourself is imperative, not only because you deserve it (as we all do) but also because you have to learn somewhere. You are your own guinea pig. Once you truly master the skills of loving and accepting yourself, you have those skills in your toolbox to offer the world.

I feel like this part of the equation is often lost by those promoting self-love. Being comfortable in your own skin by employing self-love was never meant as a "screw them! I don't care what they think!" proposition. Self-love is not meant to cause more separation. Of course, you care what they think; we're all connected, so we're meant to care what they think. Just choose whose opinions you value and take to heart.

Love requires honesty (yours and your circle's), even if it's uncomfortable. If you upset someone by promoting equality, chances are they think they're benefitting from their perception of their own superiority. You suggesting that we're all equal will topple their sense of themselves as it relates to the masses, and they probably won't really like that. It will make them feel uncomfortable. If someone likes you because they're exploiting you to cement their own false sense of identity, then you're going to want to change that, and those changes are not generally well received. Make them anyway!

When I look back on recent events in my life, I know that the devastation and subsequent growth I experienced when my ex-husband left me, equipped me with the tools I needed for the events that followed. Had I not had the benefit of going through that experience with him, more recent events probably would have had me sticking a gun in my mouth. As a result of the work I did to recover from that first devastation, I was able to cope with the next phase of my life. Appreciating the experience and how it prepared me for other events also helps me appreciate present experiences, no matter how "negative" they appear. Things may not be getting easier, but I'm getting stronger, and that leaves me in a much better place than relying on outside influences for my comfort and peace.

In the end, I would just encourage you to love. It has been said that trials and tribulations are what refine us, but love too can be a real refractory. Unconditional love is a rare and funny thing. People think they want it, but when they have the good fortune to receive it, they often treat it with doubt, disbelief, and occasionally even contempt. Then they can't figure out why their relationships don't work out and why all the "good ones" are taken. Their response to love alienates potential connections due to their own set of limiting beliefs and self-doubt, and my approach is to love anyway. Boundaries yes, conditions no. Loving regardless of the reception is indeed unconditional; letting someone walk all over you is a transgression of your boundaries. Know the difference. We are here to do the former without an attachment to the outcome. When someone loves you, you can choose to blossom and grow in the rich soil of their affection, or you can shore up your defences and don yet sturdier armour. What you can't do is stay the same. Being loved is liberating and it changes a person. If you have the good fortune to be loved, how will you choose to respond? Someone's love is a great privilege. Take it all in and be free to become the best version of yourself. Both parties are fed by this choice. Love and liberate others to give them the same opportunity.

Use the tools and examples you have been introduced to in this book to help perpetuate your relentless forward motion. Keep your journal going. Keep looking for the positive in yourself and others. Create a rock-solid foundation of self-love, respect and acceptance, and find your flow. Rest when you need to rest. Look for blessings, because it's the only way to find them. Breathe. Practice gratitude. Practice peace. When you fight, the Universe feels that energy, no matter what you're fighting for, so let go of the fight. Promote good in the world through love, not anger.

Every step you take toward growth, loving yourself and evolving changes the energy field we all live in. When you seek enlightenment, the average number of enlightened people in this world goes up. Work on yourself is work on the human race, so never doubt the importance of every positive change you make, no matter how insignificant it may seem to you.

We live in a world of superlatives, but the Universe speaks in subtleties. Learn to listen for those by quieting your surroundings outside and quieting your mind and ego-self inside. Self-doubt yells, but synchronicities whisper. They only get louder as you pay attention.

Be brave. Be here. Be love. Be a beacon. Become. Be the best version of you.

Printed in Canada